COUNTRIES OF THE MIND

SECOND SERIES

COUNTRIES OF THE MIND

ESSAYS IN LITERARY CRITICISM

By

JOHN MIDDLETON MURRY

SECOND SERIES

Essay Index Reprint Series

Originally published by:

OXFORD UNIVERSITY PRESS

BOOKS FOR LIBRARIES PRESS, INC.

FREEPORT, NEW YORK

First Published 1931
Reprinted 1968

Reprinted from a copy in the collections of
The New York Public Library
Astor, Lenox and Tilden Foundations

LIBRARY OF CONGRESS CATALOG CARD NUMBER:
68-22112

Prefatory Note

ELEVEN of these fourteen essays originally appeared in *The Times Literary Supplement*. I am grateful for permission to reprint them in this volume.

Contents

I. METAPHOR 1

II. PURE POETRY 17

III. REASON AND CRITICISM 32

IV. THE METAPHYSIC OF POETRY . . . 45

V. THE POETS' POET 63

VI. NORTH'S PLUTARCH 78

VII. SHAKESPEARE'S DEDICATION . . . 97

VIII. PROBLEMS OF THE SHAKESPEARE SONNETS 113

IX. JACQUES-BÉNIGNE BOSSUET . . . 126

X. GOTTHOLD EPHRAIM LESSING . . . 141

XI. THOMAS FLATMAN 157

XII. THE COUNTESS OF WINCHILSEA . . 166

XIII. WILLIAM GODWIN 181

XIV. CRABB ROBINSON AND THE WORDSWORTHS 188

NOTES 200

I

METAPHOR

DISCUSSIONS of metaphor—there are not many of them—often strike us at first as superficial. Not until we have ourselves made the attempt to get farther do we begin to realize that the investigation of metaphor is curiously like the investigation of any of the primary data of consciousness: it cannot be pursued very far without our being led to the borderline of sanity. Metaphor is as ultimate as speech itself, and speech as ultimate as thought. If we try to penetrate them beyond a certain point, we find ourselves questioning the very faculty and instrument with which we are trying to penetrate them. The earth trembles and yawns beneath the explorer's feet. *Medio tutissimus ibis*; but the middle way is hard to find.

Suppose we take a familiar metaphor, as that the fiery spirit of Emily Brontë burned up her body. It cannot fairly be called *cliché*; it is rather a familiar and necessary idiom. Necessary, because we find that there is no way of saying what we want to say about Emily Brontë save by this metaphor or one of its variations. This obvious necessity of the metaphor, this absence of genuine alternatives, seems to make it clear that so soon as one person perceived in another and sought to describe such a quality as Emily Brontë's, a kindred metaphor was forced upon him. We may even say that the quality could not have been perceived without the metaphor. The imagination that the soul inhabits the body as fire inhabits the material which it burns must surely go back to the moment when the existence of the soul was first surmised; for only by such an image could the nature of the soul's existence be at all apprehended. And we may leave it undecided, or as impossible of decision, whether the creation of the metaphor was the result of a search for a description of the previously felt existence of the soul, or the existence of the soul was suggested by the manner of the flame's existence.

For, whichever it may have been, and perhaps the processes were equally prevalent, metaphor appears as the instinctive and necessary act of the mind exploring reality and ordering experience. It is the means by which the less familiar is assimilated to the more familiar, the unknown to the known: it 'gives to airy nothing a local habitation and a name', so that it ceases to be airy nothing. To attempt a fundamental examination of metaphor would be nothing less than an investigation of the genesis of thought itself—a dangerous enterprise. Therefore we instinctively seek to circumscribe our own inquiries by leaving out of account as far as may be the countless host of dead or dormant metaphors of which the most part of language is composed, and concentrating upon the living ones. We take for granted the past exploration of reality of which dead and dormant metaphors are the record, and try to focus our minds on that present, hazardous, incomplete, and thrilling exploration of reality which is represented by metaphors which still retain their vitality.

Such are the metaphors of what we call creative literature. These remain alive because they are the records of an exploration of reality by men who stood head and shoulders above their fellows, who discerned resemblances between the unknown and the known which the generality could not accept nor common speech assimilate. Their metaphors are felt still to be the vehicle of some immediate revelation to those who attend to them. As Aristotle said, 'But the greatest thing of all by far is to be a master of metaphor. It is the one thing that cannot be learned from others; and it is also a sign of original genius, since a good metaphor implies the intuitive perception of the similarity in dissimilars'. The statement, made so long ago, seems final still.

But before we hazard a small attempt to advance from it towards Coleridge's discussion of imagery, we need to inquire, for the sake of clarity, whether there is any but a formal difference between metaphor and simile and image. 'Far out, as though idly, listlessly, gulls were flying. Now they settled on the waves, now they beat up into the rainy air, *and shone against the pale sky like the lights within a pearl.*' The last words would be called indifferently an image or a simile. Change them to 'shining lights in the pale pearl of sky', it becomes—not by any means to its advantage, for a reason we may discover—a metaphor. But the act of creative perception remains the same. And it seems impossible to regard metaphors and similes as different in any essential property: metaphor is compressed simile. The word 'image', however, which has come to usurp a prominent place in these discussions, is more recalcitrant. It not only narrows the content of the word 'simile', but tends to force unduly into the foreground the part played by the visual image. In the beautiful simile quoted above the visual image is preponderant; in Baudelaire's agonizing one:

Ces affreuses nuits
Qui compriment le cœur comme un papier qu'on froisse,

the visual image has no part at all. Again, it is obvious foolishness to persuade oneself that any visual image underlies the magnificent metaphors—

> Thou still unravish'd bride of quietness:
> Thou foster-child of Silence and slow Time.

Yet though the suggestion of the word 'image' is dangerous, the word is necessary. For metaphor and simile belong to formal classification. The word 'image', precisely because it is used to cover both metaphor and simile, can be used to point towards their fundamental identity; and if we resolutely exclude from our minds the suggestion that the image is solely or even predominantly visual, and allow the word to share in the heightened and comprehensive significance with which its derivative 'imagination' has perforce been endowed —if we conceive the 'image' not as primary and independent, but as the most singular and potent instrument of the faculty of imagination—it is a more valuable word than those which it subsumes: metaphor and simile. To them clings something worse than false suggestion, a logical taint, an aura of irrelevancy.

The image may be visual, may be auditory, may refer back to any primary physical experience—as those hoary metaphors which describe the process of thought itself as a grasping or apprehension—or it may be wholly psychological, the reference of one emotional or intellectual experience to another, as

> Then felt I like some watcher of the skies
> When a new planet swims into his ken . . .

The essential is simply that there should be that intuitive perception of similarity between dissimilars of which Aristotle speaks. What we primarily demand is that the similarity should be a true similarity, and that it should have lain hitherto unperceived, or but rarely perceived by us, so that it comes to us with an effect of revelation: something hitherto unknown is suddenly made known.

To that extent the image is truly creative; it marks an advance, for the writer who perceives and the reader who receives it, in the conquest of some reality.

We also in our inquiry may take a step forward. That we demand more of imagery than this may be seen in our instinctive refusal of the image of a modern prose-writer, who speaks of the 'churches, like shapes of grey paper, breasting the stream of the Strand'. There are two images, and they war with each other. If the churches really breasted the stream of the Strand, they were not at that moment like shapes of grey paper. Possibly both perceptions are valid in isolation; in association they nullify one another. Yet how often does Shakespeare seem to commit the same offence.

> It is great
> To do that thing that ends all other deeds:
> Which shackles accident, and bolts up change;
> Which sleeps, and never palates more the dug,
> The beggar's nurse and Caesar's.

Yet the offence is only apparent. The images do not in fact disturb each other, whereas the modern writer's images do. This is partly because in the modern writer's imagery the stress lies wholly upon the visual: if we do not see what we are required to see, the sentence fails of its effect; and partly because of the characteristic swiftness of Shakespeare's language. We have not, and we are not intended to have, time to unfold his metaphors; and, moreover, the boldest and most abrupt transition among them is in its effect the smoothest. For the rhythm leaves no doubt that it is not 'the dug' but Death that is 'the beggar's nurse and Caesar's'. Death, which in the previous line was the child sleeping against the heart, becomes the bosom that receives mankind. We may say it is the mere verbal suggestion that links the metaphors. Yet, though it is true that verbal 'self-suggestion' is potent in high poetry ('Forlorn! the very word is like a knell . . .'), it seems truer in this case to say that the one metaphor grows immediately out of the other. It is as though the vague 'thing', from which the images take their rise, swiftly groped after shapes before our mind's eye, and finally achieved a full realization—'the beggar's nurse and Caesar's'.

This is the work of the greatest of all masters of metaphor, and it would be preposterous to try others' achievement by its standard. The self-creative progress of Shakespeare's imagery is a thing apart. But by comparing small things with great we may see that the internal harmony which the modern writer fails to secure is a necessary quality of true imagery. Shakespeare's methods of securing it are indeed startling; he takes what seem to be impossible risks, and wins with ease. His success, when we examine it, is not really so surprising, for the extent to which images are discordant depends upon the extent to which we unfold them, and that is wholly within the great poet's control, for it in turn depends primarily upon the rhythm and tempo of his writing. And this, more than any other, is the reason why the successful use of metaphor is infinitely bolder in poetry than in prose. The poet's means of control—that is to say, the possibilities of tempo and rhythm in poetry—are infinitely richer and more flexible than in prose. He has our sensibilities, our powers of realization and comparison, far more completely under his thumb than the prose-writer. So that we may hazard a generalization and say that the creative simile is by nature more appropriate to prose than the creative metaphor. Prose gives us time to bear upon the comparison, which if it be exact and revealing, will stand the strain of our attention, and is better frankly exposed to the inquiry it must receive. And, again, the function of imagery in poetry differs perceptibly from the function of imagery in prose. In poetry metaphor is chiefly a means to excite in us a vague and heightened awareness of qualities we can best call spiritual. Exactness and precision are seldom sought, and, if they are, are seldom valuable; and often, where an apparent exactness exists, as in the Homeric simile, it is an incidental exactness and does not reinforce the point of specific analogy. Set two equally famous heroic portraits by great poets against each other.

His legs bestrid the ocean; his rear'd arm
Crested the world: his voice was propertied
As all the tunèd spheres, and that to friends;
But when he meant to quail and shake the orb,
He was as rattling thunder. For his bounty,
There was no winter in 't; an autumn 'twas
That grew the more by reaping: his delights
Were dolphin-like; they show'd his back above
The element they liv'd in: in his livery
Walk'd crowns and crownets; realms and islands were
As plates dropp'd from his pocket . . .

He above the rest
In shape and gesture proudly eminent
Stood like a Tower; his form had not yet lost
All her original brightness, nor appear'd
Less than archangel ruin'd, and th' excess
Of glory obscur'd, as when the sun new risen
Looks through the horizontal misty air
Shorn of his beams; or from behind the moon
In dim eclipse disastrous twilight sheds
On half the nations; and with fear of change
Perplexes monarchs.

The Miltonic tempo, as ever, is far slower than Shakespeare's; therefore we bear more heavily upon his comparisons, and in sufficient measure they stand the strain; but the whole effect is not precise, but rather vague, vast, and foreboding. So also, in its totally different kind, the picture of Antony that is impressed upon our minds is of some thing (rather than some one) immense, generous, genial, a careless and overflowing force of nature—a dynamic phenomenon as peculiar to Shakespeare's view of the universe as the static figure of Satan to Milton's. Exactness of this kind there is in both; but it comes not from the exactness of the particular comparisons, it is a total effect of many comparisons, as it were a painting of one great and indefinable quality by many strokes of minor yet allied analogies. To evoke such elemental spirits is seldom the purpose of prose, nor of the imagery proper to it. It also seizes, in so far as it is creative, indefinable qualities, but they are more specific and more local.

'Soon after daybreak we were steaming down the arrowy Rhone, at the rate of twenty miles an hour, in a very dirty vessel full of merchandise, and with only three or four other passengers for our companions: among whom the most remarkable was a silly old, meek-faced, garlic-eating, immeasurably polite Chevalier, with a dirty scrap of red ribbon at his buttonhole, *as if he had tied it there to remind him of something*.'

It is perfect, it gives us the man—an individual and comic inhabitant of earth. Perhaps as an example it suggests that the prose use of simile must be more prosaic than we mean to imply. We have quoted solely to point an essential difference between the imagery of prose and poetry. The imagery of poetry is in the main complex and suggestive; the imagery of prose single and explicit.

But the three examples serve also to illustrate what is

the highest function of imagery—namely, to define indefinable spiritual qualities. All metaphor and simile can be described as the analogy by which the human mind explores the universe of quality and charts the non-measurable world. Of these indefinite qualities some are capable of direct sensuous apprehension, while others can be grasped only by a faculty which, though obviously akin to sensuous apprehension, yet differs from it. Sensuous perception is of the qualities of the visible, audible, tangible world; of the spiritual qualities of the more recondite world of human personality and its creations there is intuition. Both faculties are necessary to the great poet, but there have been many who, though richly gifted with sensuous perception, have been deficient or altogether lacking in spiritual intuition. To the great poet his constant accumulation of vivid sense-perceptions supplies the most potent means by which he articulates his spiritual intuitions, for recognitions of spiritual quality can be most forcefully and swiftly conveyed through analogous recognitions of sensuous quality.[1] One has only to imagine how much, and how much in vain, another writer might toil to render the quality of Antony that is given once for all in the words, grammatically confused though they are:—

> . . . his delights
> Were dolphin-like; they show'd his back above
> The element they lived in. . . .

or to consider the pregnant subtlety of these two kindred images:

> This common body,
> Like to a vagabond flag upon the stream,
> Goes to and back, lackeying the varying tide,
> To rot itself with motion. . . .

1 See note, p. 200.

Her tongue will not obey her heart, nor can
Her heart inform her tongue,—the swan's down-feather,
That stands upon the swell at full of tide
And neither way inclines . . .

to realize the enormous resources for describing the subtlest nuances of emotion and character which a vivid percipience of the sensuous world can give.

But the greatest mastery of imagery does not lie in the use, however beautiful and revealing, of isolated images, but in the harmonious total impression produced by a succession of subtly related images. In such cases the images appear to grow out of one another and to be fulfilling an independent life of their own. Yet this apparent autonomy is as strictly subordinated to a final impression as the steps of a logical argument are to their conclusion. Such triumphs of imagery are to be conceived as a swift and continuous act of exploration of the world of imagination—though an obvious metaphor is in that phrase. A magnificent example of this peculiar movement of mind on a scale so large that it can be carefully examined is Keats's *Ode to a Nightingale*. The strange combination of imaginative autonomy and profound total harmony in that poem is characteristic of the movement of creative imagery in its highest forms. We can perhaps get a clear glimpse of the nature of this contradictory process of creative imagery—the maximum of independence combined with the most complete and pervasive subordination—in one of the rare moments when we can honestly claim to look over Shakespeare's shoulder. The famous picture of Cleopatra on Cydnus comes substantially from North's Plutarch, of which the following sentence is the original of Shakespeare's first seven lines:

'She disdained to set forward otherwise, but to take her

barge in the river of Cydnus, the poope whereof was of gold, the sails of purple, and the owers of silver, which kept stroke in rowing after the sound of flutes, howboys, cytherns, violls, and such other instruments as they played upon the barge. . . .'

It is often said that Shakespeare followed North as closely as he could, with the minimum of original effort. It is not true. North's sentence would fall quite easily into good blank verse, but it would be nothing like—

The barge she sat in, like a burnish'd throne,
Burn'd on the water: the poop was beaten gold;
Purple the sails, *and so perfumèd that*
The winds were love-sick with them; the oars were silver,
Which to the tune of flutes kept stroke, *and made*
The water which they beat to follow faster,
As amorous of their strokes. . . .

The phrases in italics are Shakespeare's additions: afterwards he keeps more closely to North, until he comes to the climax. North has it:

Others also rann out of the city to see her coming in. So that in the end, there rann such multitudes of people one after another, that *Antonius* was left post alone in the market-place, in his Imperiall seate to give audience.

Which is transformed into:

The city cast
Her people out upon her, and Antony,
Enthron'd in the market-place, did sit alone,
Whistling to the air; *which, but for vacancy,*
Had gone to gaze on Cleopatra too
And made a gap in nature.

The additions are worth attention. North's somewhat amorphous prose is given a beginning and an end. The additions are all, in spite of formal differences, essentially similes and metaphors; and, after the first, which gathers the vision into one whole which it puts imperishably before the mind's eye, the second and third develop the theme which is clinched in climax by the fourth. In them the successive elements—the winds, the water, the air—are represented all as succumbing to the enchantment of love which breathes from the great Queen and her burning barge; and by this varied return on a single motive North's inconsequential panorama is given an organic unity. It is quite impossible to conceive Shakespeare as dovetailing old and new together. Before his mind's eye as he read North had risen a picture half visible, half spiritual, in short, truly imaginative—the manifestation of Egypt, before whom the elements made obeisance. All of North that was congruous with this enchanted vision he incorporated with a flowing pen into his new creation. And the added imagery, about which he probably took no second thought, grew naturally into harmony with itself and with the whole.

To this strange but strangely natural process Coleridge was referring in his often-quoted and sometimes violently interpreted words:

> 'Images, however beautiful, though faithfully copied from nature, and as accurately represented in words, do not of themselves characterize the poet. They become proofs of original genius only in so far as they are modified by a predominant passion, or by associated thoughts and images awakened by that passion; or when they have the effect of reducing multitude to unity, or succession to an instant; or lastly when a human and intellectual life is transferred to them from the poet's own spirit.'

Instances, and better instances than Coleridge himself gives, of all the qualities which he demands of truly creative imagery are obviously to be found in the picture of Cleopatra. 'Multitude is reduced to unity' by the first of the added images; and in the other three a human and intellectual life is transferred to the images (Coleridge should perhaps have said, to the objects of the images) from the poet's own spirit. This last desideratum had been put forward long before by Aristotle in his discussion of 'vividness' in the *Rhetoric*. Vividness, he there says, depends upon metaphor and on 'setting things before the eyes'; but 'setting things before the eyes' turns out itself to be a metaphor, and not, as one might imagine, a demand for the *visual* image. 'This is my definition', says Aristotle.

'Those words set a thing before the eyes which describe it in an active state. . . . Or we may use the device often employed by Homer of giving life to lifeless things by means of metaphor. In all such cases he wins applause by describing an active state, as in the line

"Back to the plain rolled the shameless stone." '

Whether the process is described thus dryly as by Aristotle, or more transcendentally by Coleridge, as the working of the poetic spirit 'which shoots its being through earth, sea, and air', the fact is indubitable. It seems to be an imperious need of the creative spirit of the poet to impart life to the apparently lifeless. This may appear a 'device' in the cold light of analysis; but nothing is more certain than that when it is used as a device it is intolerable. No conscious contrivance produced 'Thou still unravish'd bride of quietness', or 'Joy, whose hand is ever at his lips, Bidding adieu'. Such things as these—and how many of the most magnificently natural achievements of poetry belong to this kind—are, beyond all doubt, the effect of some 'silent working of the spirit'. By the intensity of the poet's contemplation the lifeless thing lives indeed.

Probably the world of true imagination of which these

miracles are the common substance is for ever inviolable by intellectual analysis. Even to apprehend its subject-matter the intellect must suffer a sea-change, so that it is no longer itself and cannot perform its proper function. Restore its power to the intellect, again, and that which it seeks to understand has ceased to exist as what it really is. This world of imagination is a universe wherein quality leaps to cohere with quality across the abysms of classification that divide and category the universe of intellectual apprehension. Its true citizens are few and far between; they are the masters of metaphor, and the authentic messages they bring from that near yet distant country perplex our brains and comfort our souls with the half-assurance that the things that are may be otherwise than as we know them.

Towards this exalted region, as to the sole reality, Coleridge was ever groping; and what he meant by the 'predominant passion' which modifies the images of original genius is the power by which genius comprehends its chosen region of this world of qualitative interpenetration. The passion is a passionate contemplation of the unity which pervades the chosen region: a creative passion to correspond with an organic unity. Whether the unity proceeds from the passion, or the passion from the unity, it would be profitless to inquire. They are knit together, as knower and known, in one act of creative comprehension. But if we are shy of the notion of Coleridge which seems to give the poetic spirit an actually plastic power over the material world, we have only to reflect that the predominant passion of the poet's mind is but the counterpart of a predominant quality of the region of the universe which he contemplates. His passion roused by the quality is reflected back upon the quality, and gives it redoubled power; so that it begins to dominate all other qualities and properties, to suffuse them with itself till it becomes as it were the living and governing soul of that which the poet contemplates. By means of his passion the actual realizes its own idea.

However much we struggle, we cannot avoid transcendentalism, for we are seeking to approximate to a universe of quality with analogy for its most essential language through a universe of quantity with a language of identities. Sooner or later, and sooner rather than later, a transcendentalism (which is only the name for a prodigious metaphor) is inevitable. But the process may be brought a little closer to the light of common day if we take once more that region of the qualitative universe which Shakespeare embodied in Cleopatra. She was, we may say, the incarnation of love: the mighty, elemental power which, in Shakespeare's experience, was love, was made corporeal in her. She is possessed by it; from her it radiates and compels obeisance from the elements. But she is not merely a contemplated but a self-uttering thing; and this power that informs her body informs her soul also. All her thoughts are shaped by it. Without her love she will die, she must die; but when she imagines death, she imagines it as a consummation of love, as the thing

> Which sleeps, and never palates more the dug,
> The beggar's nurse and Caesar's. . . .

She dies, and her dying she imagines as a reliving of her triumph on Cydnus. 'I am again for Cydnus, to meet Mark Antony!' And it is a more wonderful triumph. 'Yare, yare, good Iras.' The flower-soft hands that yarely framed the office frame one last office more; and at the aspic's touch the Queen is wholly dedicate to the love she is and serves. The winds, the water, the air obeyed on Cydnus; now the most fickle element of all obeys—her own secret self, from which well up the images of love in death, and death in love:

> The stroke of death is as a lover's pinch
> That hurts and is desired. . . .
> Peace, peace!
> Dost thou not see my baby at my breast
> That sucks the nurse asleep?

In the intensity of Shakespeare's imagination the great property takes utter and complete possession of that it dwells in. By the alchemy of Cleopatra's images death is transmuted into a sleep of love. But her thoughts are Shakespeare's thoughts, her predominant passion his. Therefore it is not strange that Caesar, who in the waking world knows nothing of her dying words, should echo them, and prolong her triumph beyond her death.

> She looks like sleep,
> As she would catch another Antony
> In her strong toil of grace.

But Caesar did not know what Shakespeare knew, that it was the self-same Antony whom she had taken.

[1927]

II

PURE POETRY

IT is unlikely, let us hope because it is unnecessary, that there should ever be in this country the animated and even violent controversy concerning the nature of 'pure poetry' which broke out in France immediately after the Abbé Henri Bremond concluded his brilliant little lecture on that subject before the French Academy.[1] It was indeed provocative of the then latest and not the least distinguished of the 'forty' to utter so many heresies, to have talked, with the familiarity of genuine knowledge, of English poets, to have remembered the subtle definitions of the good père Rapin, to have established an affinity between the poetic and the mystical experience, and to have concluded with a refashioning of Pater's famous dictum. There was enough in the final paragraph to set the bygone immortals twittering in the shades. The magic of poetry was, he said:

'Magie recueillante, comme parlent les mystiques, et qui nous invite à une quiétude, où nous n'avons plus qu'à nous laisser faire, mais activement, par un plus grand et meilleur que nous. La prose, une phosphorescence vive et voltigeante, qui nous attire loin de nous-mêmes. La poésie, un rappel de l'intérieur, un poids confus, disait Wordsworth, une chaleur sainte, disait Keats, un poids d'immortalité sur le cœur: *an awful warmth about my heart like a load of immortality.—Amor, Pondus.*—Ce poids, où veut-il nous précipiter, sinon vers ces augustes retraites où nous attend, où

[1] LA POÉSIE PURE. Par *Henri Bremond* et *Robert de Souza*; PRIÈRE ET POÉSIE. Par *Henri Bremond*. (Paris: Grasset.)

PRAYER AND POETRY. By *Henri Bremond*. Translated by *Algar Thorold*. (Burns, Oates.)

nous appelle une présence plus qu'humaine? S'il en faut croire Walter Pater, "tous les arts aspirent à rejoindre la musique". Non, ils aspirent tous, mais chacun par les magiques intermédiaires qui lui sont propres,—les mots; les notes; les couleurs; les lignes;—ils aspirent tous à rejoindre la prière.'

Here, where we have no Academy to shock, no tradition of rationality to be offended, such a statement would pass perhaps without serious notice and certainly without serious hostility: it accords well enough both with our religious and with our poetic tradition. But in France it awakened on the one side anti-clerical fears, and on the other—more reasonably—a good-humoured suspicion: *timeo Danaos et dona ferentes.* Between the two winds of criticism the controversy was fanned into a blaze.

M. Bremond is a subtle writer, and it is not easy to make clear to ourselves precisely what he was saying; for his peroration is not quite free from ambiguity. In it he is plainly speaking of the effect of poetry upon the reader, and he is saying that 'pure poetry' induces in the well-tuned mind a condition akin to that of the silent mystical contemplation which is the supreme form of prayer. That is not equivalent to the statement which he makes elsewhere that the creation of poetry by the poet has its origin in such a state of rapture. But M. Bremond holds both these positions. There is, in the poet, a mystical or semi-mystical condition: this condition, by the magic of the words, is directly communicated to the reader. And 'pure poetry', if we understand M. Bremond correctly, is the words which allow or enforce this communication. Unfortunately, M. Bremond has linked his discussion up with a discussion by his fellow-Academician, M. Paul Valéry (whose path to a fauteuil he was eager to smooth), of a very different sort of 'pure poetry' derived from Mallarmé. The work of the pure poet in this sense of 'pure poetry' consists in the conscious and deliberate construction, upon a theme in itself utterly indifferent, of a musical pattern of words which gives delight. In this sense the 'purity' of poetry consists in its absolute independence of subject: 'pure poetry' is simply verbal 'music'. This conception, by which we have not been greatly troubled in England, despite M. Valéry's authentic ancestor, Edgar Allan Poe, has no necessary connexion with M. Bremond's; and it is a pity that M. Bremond did not more sharply distinguish between them.

M. Bremond's position is a little obscured, not only by his references to M. Valéry's very definite and very different theory of 'pure poetry', but by his Catholic orthodoxy. His appreciation of poetry is so intense that he is inevitably tempted to represent the poet as a Christian mystic who has, so to speak, at the crucial moment taken the wrong turning. Instead of surrendering himself to the silent ecstasy of communion with God, the poet is lured by the demon of expression into utterance of the unutterable. One may point out—indeed, M. Bremond himself lightly indicates as much—that most Christian mystics appear to have been troubled by a similar demon, who lured them into utterance that was not always poetry; consequently, if poets are mystics *manqués*, so are most mystics; and finally, whereas mystics sometimes squander their beatitudes in verbiage, poets do at least produce from them the thing of beauty and the joy for ever. In other words, it may be orthodoxy and not the poets to whom the attitude of *timeo Danaos* in face of M. Bremond's theory would be the more appropriate.

But these are consequences only if the theory be

accepted. It needs a closer investigation first. The argument upon which M. Bremond mainly depends to establish a relation between the mystical and the poetic experience is the familar one that the notional or rational content of a line of true poetry is not of prime importance to its poetic quality. M. Bremond goes further and declares that the notional content is absolutely irrelevant to the poetic quality. He gives for an instance the famous (though perhaps legendary) correction by Keats of 'A thing of beauty is a constant joy' into the first line of *Endymion*. The notional content of the two lines is hardly distinguishable: yet one is poetry, and the other not. Through one, to use M. Bremond's homely metaphor, the current passes; through the other there is no transmission. We must conclude therefore two things: first, that poetry is words by which something is communicated from the poet to the reader, and, second, that this something communicated is not a mere notion or an idea. What is it? Tolstoy said 'an emotion'; Signor Croce says, 'an intuition'; M. Bremond says an incomplete mystical experience; Professor Whitehead, if we understand him rightly, a fragment of the concrete real of primary experience. And, of course, there are innumerable other answers, with innumerable nuances of difference.

What seems most important to have clearly in mind is that the problem is not at all peculiar to poetry in the common sense of the word; it is simply the problem of that 'magic of style' which Matthew Arnold declared to be 'creative' of vision and understanding and virtue in the reader. Perhaps, had M. Bremond been less enchanted by the particular vistas which his approach to the problem seemed to open up, and had he faced it in its full universality as the crux of creative style, he could have gone to the prose-writers of his own country for some less fitful, and less startling, illumination. Stendhal's lucid apophthegm might have warned him against too quick, or too Tolstoyan, a denial that the element of thought in poetry is more than an accidental concomitant of the pure poetry. 'Le style,' said Stendhal, 'est ceci: ajouter à une pensée donnée toutes les circonstances propres à produire tout l'effet que doit produire cette pensée.' Whatever the limitations of the dictum, it seems to throw more light than a directly mystical theory on the nature of the process by which Keats transformed 'A thing of beauty is a constant joy' into 'A thing of beauty is a joy for ever'. In both lines the thought is the same; but in the second the harmony of words in which it is expressed enables the thought to produce its full and true effect. There are difficulties in Stendhal's explanation which must be faced; but it takes more account of the facts than any theory which tends to regard the element of thought in poetry as completely irrelevant to it.

We must guard ourselves against pressing the explanation too hard, and remember that 'thought' in Stendhal's vocabulary meant very much more than logical notions or distinct concepts; again, we must be prepared to find that the quantity of distinguishable thought in poetry varies infinitely. The line of Keats, being positively gnomic, is not representative; nor is perhaps the line of Shakespeare, with its elusive thought content,

> After life's fitful fever he sleeps well.

But it brings us by a shade nearer to Stendhal's essential meaning. Every 'thought', at least of those thoughts with which poetry is concerned, has its emotional context, or 'field'. The thoughts which have no emotional 'field' are by nature alien to poetry. Thoughts which for one man may appear to be without an emotional 'field' may be greatly charged with it for another, as, for instance, the Epicurean metaphysic for Lucretius, or the Ptolemaic astronomy for Dante. The full effect that the thought *ought* to produce is, therefore, not absolute; it means the effect that the thought does produce upon the poet's mind, and which, from his point of view, it ought to produce upon the mind of his reader. Poetry will, therefore, be words which do communicate a 'thought' and the emotional 'field' which it excites from the mind of the poet to the mind of the reader.

We may advance a little further. It is obvious that the 'thought' and its emotional 'field' are inseparable from one another; for the emotional 'field' is none other than what happens in the thinking of the thought: it is, we might even say, the actual *thinking* of the thought. Assuredly, the thought and the emotional field are not more distinct than faintly discernible aspects of a single and entire mental act. It would be, in fact, extremely hazardous to say even that the thought came before the emotional 'field'; whatever priority it may have is logical and not actual. And, as a matter of fact, there is good reason for believing that in the activity of many great poets the emotional field is actually prior to the thought, which is, as it were, a condensation of an emotional atmosphere.[1] By this line of approach we preserve what truth there is in M. Bremond's metaphor of 'the current that passes', and avoid what seems to us his premature and dangerous separation of thought and the specifically poetic in poetry. We are not under the illusion that we have explained anything; we have simply prevented a false simplification. Against our caution

[1] See note, p. 200.

M. Bremond might adduce once more the line dear to Marcel Proust and himself,

> La fille de Minos et de Pasiphaë

and once again deny that it contains any thought whatever. To which we must reply that such an absolute negation of thought is untrue to the fact. The line is not mere incantation any more than is

> Jousted in Aspramont, or Montalban.

In both there is an evident distinguishment of quality—exotic rich and rare in both: in Racine's line soft and languorous, in Milton's clangorous and martial. To deny to such a discernment of quality the name of thought would be either to degrade nearly the whole of our mental activity to mere sensation, or to exalt it, unnecessarily and quite improbably, to mystic communion with the ineffable. It would be, we think, altogether more becoming and more convincing to admit that the range of mental acts in poetry is unlimited, and that the element of distinguishable thought can vary from a comprehensive proposition—'We are such stuff as dreams are made on'—to the most tenuous apprehension of a quality physical, or spiritual, or both—'the plainsong cuckoo gray'. What is essential is that the 'thought' should be an intrinsic part of an emotional field in the poet's mind, and that a corresponding emotional field should be excited in ourselves.

There is plenty of mystery in poetry without making it mystical. And we may, perhaps, advance a step further and suggest that the poet is he in whom the vast majority of his 'thoughts'—in the large sense invoked above—occur with vivid emotional fields. It is probably true that in the mental activity of even the ordinary run of men thoughts are always accompanied by such emotional fields, but that they ignore them. They have the best reason for ignoring them, because they have no means of distinguishing them from one another. The poet, on the contrary, from the beginning, possesses such a means. He has the Word. The word in the poet's mind partly arises out of the emotional field, partly is deliberately fitted to convey it. This mating of the word to the entire mental experience of thought and emotional field experienced as one is the specific poetic act. If an ordinary man were visited by Prospero's thought, which came, we may remember, to a troubled brain and a beating mind, he would strive to remember it. He would not be able to remember it. He might say: 'An extraordinary thought came to me. We are like dreams'. Then he would hesitate, knowing that he had betrayed his thought, and add wistfully, 'But it was beautiful'. No doubt it was; but the beauty is lost for ever, for the beauty lay not in the thought, but in the thinking of the thought with its inseparable ambience of the emotion in which it was conceived and of which it was the consummation. In order that the beauty should be saved from the iniquity of oblivion it is necessary not that the thought should be expressed, but that the entire mental experience—thought and emotional field—should be fixed in words:

We are such stuff
As dreams are made on; and our little life
Is rounded with a sleep.

Into the means by which this communication of an entire mental experience is made possible it would be fascinating, though perhaps unprofitable, to inquire. At this point we seem to have reached an ultimate. But we have reached it, in despite of M. Bremond's orthodox enchantments, without recourse to mysticism. No *deus* (*ex machina* or immanent) has any aid to give. Some poets may think about God—perchance they may experience Him—but other poets have done neither one nor the other; but all are poets if they have the power so to mate the word to an entire mental experience that its similar is aroused in their readers. By virtue of that power alone they are 'pure poets' and their words 'pure poetry'. Whether they are great poets or not is an entirely different question, which will depend upon the value we assign to the entire mental experiences which they communicate to us. But we may say this: it is impossible that a 'pure poet' should be bad. The question we may have to decide is simply the degree of his goodness. Good in essence he must be.

For, as we have tried to suggest, poetry is not what some have (in intention, rightly) maintained it is—namely, communication—whether of mere emotion, which would be sheer sensation, or of mere thought. It is the communication of an entire experience. And this, whether we approve or not, as moral beings, of the experience which is communicated to us, is an awakening for us. We remember what we have failed to remember; we experience what we did not experience, because we could not distinguish it; and above all we are brought into direct and complete communion with another and more gifted human being. His thoughts are our thoughts, and his ways our ways, though it may be for a moment only; and his ways, in one essential, and that one essential by which he is a poet, are better than our ways; for he does realize and possess his experience in its wholeness. He does not, *qua* poet, abstract from it or mutilate it. Whether his thought be what we should ordinarily call a thought, or what we should ordinarily call a perception, he possesses it in its whole living actuality, and not as a vague schema or skeleton. It is rich with its own emotional flesh and blood. It is warm experience. Further, it seems to follow that it is an obvious misnomer to call this experience, which the poet possesses and communicates, either emotional experience or intellectual experience. Either name involves a radical impoverishment of the experience itself; it is neither the one nor the other. Nor again is it both together. It is itself one thing, *sui generis*. We can no more separate its two elements of soul and body in the more familiar unity of the living man, to which the unity of the poetic experience has evident and suggestive analogies.

So that the primary and essential beneficence of poetry is that it recreates in any well-tuned sensibility an organic unity of mental experience of which man in his ordinary moments is deprived. Like the quality of mercy, it 'is not strained. It blesseth him that gives and him that takes'. Hence, and not from any doubtful translunary sources, that 'magie recueillante, où nous n'avons plus qu'à nous laisser faire', of which M. Bremond speaks. And when he adds 'mais activement', we shall agree; but when he adds yet further 'par un plus grand et meilleur que nous', we shall shake our heads without regret. The one who is greater and better than ourselves is simply the poet, who communicates to us the unity of his own inward experience, and by so doing, and as an essential condition of so doing, momentarily creates in us a unity of inward experience which is indefeasibly our own. Hence comes that strange 'note' of the poetic experience which men of genius so diverse as Keats and Tolstoy have insisted upon, that 'it should be a wording of our own highest thoughts *and come to us almost as a remembrance*'. It comes to us, in simple verity, not almost, but quite, as a remembrance; at the touch of the poetic experience we become that which we are and which we were not—momentarily whole. Intellect and emotion, mind and heart, regain their lost unity within us.

If, then, 'pure poetry' is simply words which communicate to or stimulate in us the organic entirety of an experience, it has still to stand before the bar of a final judgement. That we should be enabled, through pure poetry, to receive a mental experience in its wholeness and, as a necessary condition of this reception, to experience it anew is an indubitable good. We gain a positive enrichment and integration; we might say, if the phrase were not hampered with theological and metaphysical obligations—'servitudes' would be the proper word—that we are put, if not into possession of, at least into touch with, our souls. To avoid the servitudes we must be content to claim a momentary union of thought and feeling. That will always be, relatively to our normal and necessary dissociations, joyful and beneficent. But the problems of life remain. High speculations still confront the serious spirit; and though it may catch from the plenitude of any actual experience received and achieved through poetry some surmise of ultimate attainment, it cannot be satisfied with an experience less than that of which it is itself potentially capable. Its own high speculations, its own moral bewilderments, must have place in a poetic experience that shall be adequate to its own potentiality. Those 'thoughts on nature and on human life' which Matthew Arnold so earnestly desiderated are indeed to be required of the poet who is to receive his guerdon, not merely of poetical 'purity', but of poetical 'greatness' also. But we on our part are required to remember that there is already implicit in pure poetry at the simplest level of perceptive experience a thought on nature and on human life which is both pregnant and elusive. For it does assure us that an act of simple perception, if it could be held in its uncontaminated wholeness, as the poet holds it for us, is at once ultimate and satisfying. For the term of its own existence it completely engages the spiritual being; it brings us indeed into that 'fellowship with essence' than which, while we enjoy it, we can ask no more. To whatever extremity of demand upon poetry our moral being may lead us we must not forget that the simplest fragment of pure poetry has its own metaphysical and moral finality. It may not enshrine our highest thoughts, but it will have enshrined our purest thoughts: and purity is an ultimate category. Nevertheless, we are what we are, and we demand from poetry, if it shall be great, thoughts that are not merely pure but high. The poet, being a man of like passions with ourselves, also demands it of himself. Sometimes high thinking is not for him; we feel that we could think better than he does, and he is not for us a great poet. Sometimes his high thoughts and ours seem marvellously at one; and then, since he has enabled us to possess our own thoughts, not as we usually possess them, at once in the mechanic hardness of definition and the ambient vagueness of the undefined, but in their warm immediacy with all the wholeness of activity which distinguishes thoughts from ratiocinations, he is for us a great poet. Than this there is no more than any man can do for us. If more could be done, we should be incapable of receiving it.

But again we need to be on our guard. The high thoughts of poetry can be experienced only through poetry. We ought not to come to the poet saying: 'Such and such are high and true thoughts. These you must think.' Doing thus we should fall, as many high-thinking critics have fallen, into the mistake of Plato, without his awareness of his act. We have to remember that we may not know what high and true thoughts may be, and that this also the poet may have to reveal to us. The thought of the futility of human life—who shall say whether or not that thought is *true*? It is one which the well-tuned man would rather not believe to be true; and yet, when he has listened to Macbeth:

> To-morrow, and to-morrow, and to-morrow,
> Creeps in this petty pace from day to day,
> To the last syllable of recorded time ;
> And all our yesterdays have lighted fools
> The way to dusty death. Out, out, brief candle!
> Life's but a walking shadow, a poor player
> That struts and frets his hour upon the stage,
> And then is heard no more; it is a tale
> Told by an idiot, full of sound and fury,
> Signifying nothing;

—something is changed. There are undreamed-of riches, it seems, even in an ultimate despair; a glory is shed over the road to dusty death. This despair is not despairing, because it is complete. The act of the poet's mind has thrilled the poet's heart.

Here perhaps we touch upon the hidden nature of the high thought of poetry. Those acts of the mind must thrill the heart. If our own high thoughts thrill our hearts, it is well with us, for even though we lack the gift of utterance we are poets in mind: we explore life with all we are, we receive our thoughts into the depth of us, or drag them out of it. But we can and do demand of poetry even more than this. We demand that the high thoughts of poetry should not merely thrill, but also still our hearts. Which of the great poets will succeed most intimately with us in this respect depends upon our spiritual and mental condition. Many men are so constituted that religion is not enough for them; it must be a religion. Such a man will find in Dante's line, 'E la sua volontate è nostra pace' a finality and therefore a completeness of satisfaction which he would not find in

> Men must endure
> Their going hence, even as their coming hither:
> Ripeness is all.

Another, less apt to the mysteries of the Christian religion, will find this peace in the Shakespeare. While yet another will find them equal in potency, and believe that the act of soul, the loving surrender of the heart to the high thought of the mind, in both is indistinguishable. But no matter to which persuasion we belong, we shall insist that these supreme felicities belong to those poets alone who have thought long and deeply on the inevitable mysteries of life and, being poets indeed, have refused an answer which left any part of themselves unresponsive.

To men such as these the debt of humanity is inestimable. They, above all others, keep the souls of men alive; they do not tell us of spiritual felicity, they create it in us from the substance of our coarser elements. Christianity itself lives—by whatever means it may exist—by the magic of the poetry of Christ. From his high poetry Dante's magical line was directly caught. Shakespeare no less responded to it; witness the unfaltering quality of his words whenever Christ or Christianity is glanced at even sidelong by his verse. That is simply because the essence of Christianity is the utterance of a pure and morally great poetic nature; and in this order like must be attuned to like. Not that Shakespeare was a Christian, any more than the poet is a mystic. But he was religious, as all great poets must be. For high poetry and high religion are at one in the essential that they demand that a man shall not merely think thoughts, but feel them—that his highest mental act be done with all his heart and with all his mind and with all his soul.

[OCTOBER 1928

III

REASON AND CRITICISM

The comparative quiescence of the creative spirit in our literature of recent years has found a certain compensation in the increased activity of the critical. That the body of serious criticism has grown in the last dozen years is evident to a sober survey. Criticism may be less popular, but it is more critical; and to that extent may fairly be held to supply a counterpoise to creative barrenness. For criticism that is critical is the expression of a real spiritual energy and the satisfaction of a real spiritual need. It is autonomous. That is not to say merely that criticism is the satisfaction of an individual's need for self-expression, which is obvious enough, but that it is not a secondary and derivative means of self-expression. In creative periods it may be apparently true that, as Dryden said, the corruption of a poet is the generation of a critic; but the reality, as Dryden himself signally proved, is that in a creative period the poet himself is the best critic.

If we may talk of periods at all, we are now in a critical period. The most forceful, the most creative literary intelligences of to-day have a bias towards criticism. It may be true that they are also lacking in energy; but their critical preoccupations derive most directly from their own awareness of this lack of energy, and of the extraordinary demands upon their fund of energy made by the social and spiritual disintegration of the age. To create significantly, Tolstoy once said, an artist must be on a level with the highest life-conception of his age. That position was not so hard to achieve fifty, even twenty, years ago; the artist could acquire it almost unconsciously. But to-day the situation is very different: there is no predominant life-conception which commands the adherence of the spiritual *élite*, if a snobbish expression may be used without snobbish intention. The artist who would be significant has first painfully to work out his own synthesis of experience, beginning from utter nakedness; nothing is *given* to him. What wonder if all his energies are employed in making a garment for himself when he has to build his loom and spin his thread?

Creation there is, of course, and creation in plenty, but it is seldom significant. It is based on either a naïve and ignorant, or a deliberate and labour-saving, exclusion of significant experience. For this sufficient reason contemporary criticism is but little concerned with contemporary creation, which it criticizes implicitly by ignoring; and that is a sufficient reply to those who inveigh against contemporary criticism for its lack of interest in the present. Because it is really interested in the present, and the future in the present, it turns aside from the irrelevance of so much contemporary creation. It has positive work to do; and to confuse positiveness with actuality, or 'news-value', is one of the most alarming symptoms of that disintegration against which modern criticism is dispersedly but pertinaciously striving. To justify literature—this is the object and aim of modern criticism. Thus stated, it seems either quixotic or otiose. It may be said, literature happens. That nowadays it does very little else is the gravamen common to all serious criticism. This criticism is well aware that no possible legislation can control the birth of the εὐφυὴς ἢ μανικός; but it insists that something can be done to make him εὐφυής rather than μανικός when once he has been born. This possible something is the re-elaboration of a system of values, the determination of the question whether literature is a sort of pastime or at best a private and esoteric religion—and eventually the creation of a common consciousness of literary responsibility which may serve as a palaestra for the right exercise of genius in happier days to come.

To this work Mr. Herbert Read has made a valuable contribution in his book of essays.[1] Their scope and purpose is not quite adequately indicated in the title *Reason and Romanticism*, which may suggest that the author is engaged in positing anew the old and barren opposition between classicism and romanticism. Though there are moments when Mr. Read himself seems to give colour to this view of his undertaking, most of his pages are animated by a more generous breath, and are made exciting, and perhaps also a little elusive, by his effort towards a new synthesis. He avowedly finds the pattern of it in an old one, in the system of St. Thomas Aquinas, though we wonder sometimes whether his nearer inspiration should not be sought in Mr. Santayana, of whom, to our surprise, Mr. Read has little to say.

A new synthesis is a vague and, as used in late years, an ultra-romantic expression. We had best establish as clearly as we can the elements Mr. Read seeks to synthesize. He holds, in common with many others, that the old religious nexus of European civilization has been finally destroyed:

'The criticism of revealed religion has been operative not only on the empirical plane (which matters little) but also on the psychological plane. A religion like Christianity is built up largely of unconscious symbols: it finds its most powerful forces in subconscious processes, like prayer, grace,

[1] Reason and Romanticism: Essays in Literary Criticism. By *Herbert Read*. (Faber and Gwyer.)

and faith. The effect of experimental science has been to destroy the unconsciousness of these symbols: it understands them and therefore equates them with conscious equivalents, which are no longer symbols, and which on that account no longer compel the imagination.'

It may be remarked in passing that the word 'subconscious' in the second of these sentences comes strangely from the pen of a Thomist. Perhaps it is a little more difficult than Mr. Read imagines to be a Thomist when you have abolished one term of the Thomist synthesis, which was between religion and science. For some cause, moreover, Mr. Read is a little shy of stating explicitly what is to take the place of religion in the new synthesis. It is, of course, literature. 'Science and Poetry have but one ideal, which is the satisfaction of the Reason.' At which the scientist, at least, will prick up his ears. What does Mr. Read mean by reason? It is, as he truly says, 'a very difficult word to use without confusion'.

> 'It is often used as a synonym for rationality, or even for a mechanistic logic. Reason should rather connote the widest evidence of the senses, and of all processes and instincts developed in the long history of man. It is the sum total of awareness, ordained and ordered to some specific end or object of attention.'

The logician may make merry over that definition, not we. On the contrary, we heartily approve of the breadth of connotation Mr. Read seeks to give to the much-disputed word. However much he may abjure the epithet, we welcome him as a true humanist, for whom reason is rather a condition than a faculty. To possess reason is to have achieved an ordered and comprehensive experience. To this ordered and comprehensive experience science and poetry alike make their appeal, and by it they are judged.

But, it may be asked, why should the religious experience be denied a place in this ordered sum total of human awareness which is reason? Even if we accept Mr. Read's contention that the Christian symbolism has ceased to be valid, how does it follow that the mode of experience which found satisfaction in these symbols has ceased to exist? Are the experiences that were once called prayer and grace and faith no longer realities for the enlightened mind because it has reduced them, or believes it has reduced them, to subjective attitudes? It is just at this point that we should be grateful for a little more clarity in Mr. Read's exposition. We surmise, but we cannot be sure, that his aim is to transfer the religious response to literature and art. The religious experience, criticized and ordered by the intellect, will still hold its place in reason, but its mode of expression is changed. Into what, again we cannot precisely determine; but it seems that Mr. Read's solution is adumbrated in his interesting essay on 'The Nature of Metaphysical Poetry', which he describes as 'the emotional apprehension of thought'. Whether or not this description is too wide (for it would cover a good deal of poetry which Mr. Read would not, or would not yet, admit to be 'metaphysical'), it suggests that his ideal reconciliation of religion and science and poetry is in a sort of Aristotelian *θεωρία*. We should have to go to Mr. Santayana for a lucid statement of the ideal.

'In philosophy investigation and reasoning are only preparatory and servile parts, means to an end. They terminate in insight, or what in the noblest sense of the word may be called 'theory', *θεωρία*—a steady contemplation of all things in their order and worth. Such contemplation is imaginative. No one can reach it who has not enlarged his mind and tamed his heart. A philosopher who attains it is, for the moment, a poet; and a poet who turns his trained and practised imagination on the order of all things, or on anything in the light of the whole, is for the moment a philosopher.'

Such a contemplation could be called indifferently poetic, philosophic, or religious. The essential of its attainment is that process of self-discipline which Mr. Santayana describes as an enlargement of the mind and a taming of the heart—or, in more schematic terms, that the man whose nature it is to advance by one of the three paths should at all times be mindful of the existence of the other two and accustom himself to reach the same position by working along them.

Mr. Read himself comes nearest to an explicit formulation of this ideal in some admirable words on 'the universal mind', which he puts forward as the ideal type of the critical mind.

'It has been a common saying, since Pope first said it, that a little learning is a dangerous thing. But far more dangerous is the learning which, though not little, is limited. It is idle to think that any good can come of a specialization that is not linked to some wider ethos, itself the product of a versatile intelligence, or that is not subordinate to general wisdom. And this applies not only to the scientist whom we regard rather rashly as the only specialist, but equally to the critic and the poet. A general idea, whether it be a new image or a new hypothesis, invariably springs across two hitherto widely separated concepts: it is the electric spark that plays suddenly *before* contact is made between approaching poles of magnetism. Only a universal mind is likely to contain these pairs of opposites, and for that single reason (and apart from the question of general wisdom) the universal mind alone is capable of "creative" thought. It may be said that this is an impossible ideal: that the rare occurrence of a universal mind, as in Aristotle, Dante, Leibniz, or Goethe, is the definite result of a *lusus naturae*—of chance, in fact. But the universal mind is not necessarily of this order, and universality is a quality possessed by all the rarer spirits of any age: it is a quality I would ascribe, not merely to Aristotle and Leibniz, but to Lucian, Diderot, and Ruskin, as well as to Emily Brontë. It does not mean the possession of all knowledge, or even, necessarily, of any knowledge at all. It does imply a capacity *to receive* all knowledge and events with equanimity and unprejudiced percipience; and to build up a positive attitude on this clear and serene perceptual basis.'

That is excellently said; and it is to be remarked how close this ideal of the critical mind is to the ideal of the creative mind. Indeed, Mr. Read has already identified them by saying that the universal mind alone is capable of creative thought; and when he passes on to describe the potentially universal mind he comes as near as he may to identifying it with that 'experiencing nature' which Bagehot posited as the primary endowment of the creative writer. Yet, strangely enough, among the names which Mr. Read singles out we do not find Shakespeare, to whom Goethe of the universal mind ascribed a universality immeasurably greater than his own. And the omission, set beside the inclusion of Dante, is surely deliberate.

It is significant that this striking omission should correspond with what we can only call a bias towards intellectualism which, in spite of intermittent repression, emerges continually through this book. In the abstract Mr. Read sees clearly enough that the reason which he champions is of a higher order than any intellectualism; more remarkably still, when he comes to the specific exercise of his critical powers, as in the brilliant essays on Smollett and on Charlotte and Emily Brontë, his judgement is quite free from this bias. Nevertheless, in his more general discussions his comprehensive and creative conception of reason tends steadily to narrow in scope and to become purely discursive and conceptual. In his essay on metaphysical poetry he manages to superinduce in himself that uncritical frame of mind for which verse that contains a maximum of explicit conceptual thought becomes superior to poetry that is mindful of its proper function and excellence—namely, to pursue its rhythmic progress through an identity of image and idea. He becomes for the moment unable to distinguish between a mere transposition of discursive thinking into the form of poetry and the organic sequence of embodied intuitions which gives to great poetry its peculiar and inimitable design. This leads him greatly to overpraise Donne and to fail to recognize that Donne's glaring deficiencies in 'architectonic' are the confession of failure of a mind that was almost as undisciplined as it was active. 'Exactitude and all the last conditions of form,' said Goethe, 'can just as well accompany the formless, as the truly formed.' And Donne's exactitude is of this deceptive kind.

In spite, therefore, of his clear theoretic appreciation of the distinction, Mr. Read comes very near to confusing reason with intelligence. His own search for a precise terminology has had the unexpected effect of making him more liable to the error than of safeguarding him against it. Poetry, he says at the end of a rather caustic criticism of Mr. George Moore's anthology of 'Pure Poetry', is to be judged 'by the quality of intelligence inherent in the poem'. 'But what,' he rightly anticipates our asking, 'is intelligence?' And he replies:

'It is a question I have tried to answer generally in this book; here it will be sufficient to say that it is the same faculty of "direct apprehension" already distinguished by mediaeval philosophy, and since then somewhat compromised, in differing degrees, by Descartes, Spinoza, and Bergson. It is dangerous perhaps to describe it as a "faculty", for it is in reality but one aspect of the single faculty of apprehension. It is perhaps only the distinction between reason which is concentrated on a single object and reason which is discursive. It is a distinction clearly and for all time made by no less an authority than St. Thomas Aquinas: "intelligere enim est simpliciter veritatem intelligibilem apprehendere: ratiocinari autem est procedere de uno intellecto ad aliud, ad veritatem intelligibilem cognoscendam." '

The distinction may have been made clearly and for all time, but to a modern mind the word 'intelligence' does not connote the faculty or act of 'simple apprehension of truth'. To a modern mind that act or faculty is 'intuition'. Whether we know as much as we ought to know about intuition may be doubted, but we shall not increase our knowledge by calling it intelligence. We shall only wander in a maze of misunderstandings. Synthesis is certainly desirable, but we shall pay too heavy a price for it if we are to be required to confound realities which are different.

Mr. Read's problem, which he has not solved but has rather concealed from himself, is to determine the nature of 'intuition'. His reference to the statement and authority of St. Thomas settles nothing; in fact it brings him only to a position identical with that of Signor Croce, for whom intuitions are primary perceptions—the elements of thought. But such intuitions are obviously not the intuitions with which we are concerned in a great poem. These are not primary and direct perceptions, but complex and elaborate attitudes to whose formation both sense-perceptions and thought-intuitions have contributed; and, though it would be true to say that the validity and worth of the work depend upon the degree to which it satisfies the reason, in Mr. Read's largest interpretation of the word, it is not to be forgotten that this satisfaction of the reason (in the case of a true work of art) is discovered well after the experience. The great poem acts like a magnet on the paper of iron filings; it *creates* a new order in our experience, and itself enlarges our conception of reason. It may give some small stay to our hunger for schematism to assimilate this mysterious operation of the work of literature to the direct and simple apprehension of the truth of an axiom of Euclid, but in reality they are very different; and by insisting upon this premature identification we run a serious risk of exaggerating the purely intellectual element in the work of literature and of demanding from it a quality that it does not, and ought not to, possess.

For if, as we with Mr. Read believe, reason is ordered experience and the highest reason is the most comprehensive experience rightly ordered, what grounds have we for supposing that this order is an intellectual order? There is observable in the great province of life to which we human beings belong another kind of order than the geometric or intellectual; there is organic order. And that is the kind of order we should naturally suppose to be appropriate to human experience. That also is the kind of order we find in the highest literature. We cannot say, even in the simplest instance, that we 'understand' an organism; neither ought we to say that we must abjure our understanding ('plunge into the life-stream') to apprehend it; rather, perhaps, that we must transcend our understanding. Transcend is a dangerous word; but we are forced to use some term to designate the middle path between understanding and nescience. The middle path exists; it is positive and autonomous. It is that which Pascal strove to distinguish when he contrasted the *esprit de finesse* with the *esprit de géométrie*. May we not hazard the conjecture that it alone can truly be called the path of reason? It is not easy to discover or to tread. The temptation to reduce reason to understanding is persistent, and the consequences of surrendering to it, for the individual and for society alike, pernicious. For the feelings, as Coleridge said, 'will set up their standard against the understanding, whenever the understanding has renounced its allegiance to the reason'. That is the explanation of the extravagances of romanticism in the large history of the human spirit. But the function of the individual is to overcome this secular antimony in himself. The insurgence of feeling against the understanding, the war of the romantic against the classic, is no less an individual than a social condition. But neither side will ever gain a victory that is permanent; the true, the positive, the creative outcome of the struggle is a harmonious unity. The intelligence as such will never succeed in controlling the emotions, only in killing them: 'le cœur a ses raisons . . .' It is reason that should control both.

Yet the notion of control is itself misleading and irrelevant. Reason is born of the pregnant opposition between intelligence and feeling, Mind and Heart; and they exist no longer in themselves, but in their offspring.[1] There is a complete interfusion of understanding and emotion, so that both are different in nature from what they were before. This organic evolution of the consciousness which both Goethe and Coleridge strove, not

[1] See note p. 200.

wholly in vain, to describe and to communicate finds its appropriate object of contemplation in an organic universe: to this end indeed was it born, and from the failure of the effort to accommodate emotional experience of the living world, within and without, to intellectual categories, it took its origin. Reason is the understanding of life.

Of this possible condition wherein, by virtue of the organic order achieved within the individual consciousness, a comprehension of the organic order of human experience is attained, the manifold complex and harmonious satisfactions of the great work of literature are, as it were, premonitory. More than that, they are directly creative of it. A great work of literature does not so much satisfy the reason as bring it to birth within ourselves. We experience its potency long before we can appreciate the worth and significance of the experience; it works in ways beyond our conscious control. To seek consciously to control it is a temptation and an error: we succeed only in making ourselves immune from its beneficent operation. But once we know, by subtle and unmistakable signs, that a creative contact has been established, that our experience has become, in a single moment, both richer and more serene, then it is our manifest duty to bring the details of the strange process into the full light of our consciousness. Only thus can we consolidate our position on the heights that genius has won for us. The man who leaves the poetic experience as an isolated miracle is not merely uncritical, he is not truly alive. He must, for his own sake, co-ordinate it. But this co-ordination cannot be accomplished by reducing the experience to an intellectual category which it transcended. We have been granted a moment of the pure life of Reason; it is our duty not to degrade it into a function of our ordinary consciousness, but to seek a way to lift our ordinary consciousness to the condition we have been privileged to share. It is, after all, not an alien condition, but our own, because we have been proved capable of it.

[JULY 1926

IV

THE METAPHYSIC OF POETRY

In a recent essay Sir Henry Newbolt discussed the conceptions of Time and Eternity that have found expression in poetry, and in conclusion, with the aid of some rather difficult speculations by the late Dr. McTaggart, tried to indicate a path of thought which (he believed) might lead some future poet to a more comfortable creed concerning these high subjects and so to a more comforting achievement. The light of a new dawn glimmers, for Sir Henry Newbolt, in Dr. McTaggart's contention that 'events in Time take place in an order—a fixed and irrevocable order. But there is in the mere form of Time itself nothing to determine what this order shall be'.

'What then does determine the order of events in Time, on the supposition that Time is only an illusory way of regarding a timeless reality? The philosopher believes that there is good reason to hold that the order is determined by the adequacy with which the states represent the eternal reality, so that those states come next together which only vary infinitesimally in the degree of their adequacy.'

Dr. McTaggart (according to Sir Henry Newbolt) held that he was justified in believing that the representations of reality presented to us in the time series are becoming more and more adequate, and will continue inevitably to do so until 'we reach the last stage in the series, and enter upon the perfect vision which lies beyond time'. An inspiring philosophic faith which, if a future poet were to embrace, 'surely his poetry would have the power to give, as only poetry can give, consolation and encouragement in the evils of the present'.

I doubt it—for many reasons. The simplest of them is that I cannot understand the theory. Perhaps, in the long practice of literary criticism, what little metaphysic wit I once possessed has worn away; but I can make nothing even of the primary notion that, though events in Time take place in fixed and irrevocable order, 'there is in the mere form of Time itself nothing to determine what this order shall be'. What is this 'mere form of Time' that can be thus abstracted from events? The events in their order are our datum: the category or form of Time is derived from our contemplation of them. Time without events, events without Time, both are inconceivable. And, since my earth-bound wings refuse this first flight into the empyrean, the subsequent speculation upon the growing 'adequacy' of events in the time series to the eternal reality remains as remote from me, and as impotent to console me (did I need consolation), as the farthest of the fixed stars; nor can I imagine that any poetry which accepted and proclaimed such a theory would have more potency over me.

Not, at all events, in virtue of its theory. In virtue of the passion of mind with which the imaginary poet embraced it, perhaps. I am totally unmoved by the cosmology of Epicurus, deeply thrilled by the response it awakened in the mind of Lucretius, for there I find a secular passion of the human soul—to be freed from blind ancestral fears—uttered with a constrained intensity of emotion. And, no doubt, if the imaginary poet were to find in Dr. McTaggart's theory a deliverance from a spiritual bondage comparable to that once experienced by Lucretius, his pent-up soul might leap to a like magnificence of contemplative rapture. But it is improbable that he would bring much more comfort to his readers than Lucretius has brought to his. Yet Lucretius was passionately convinced that he was bringing a message of hope to his fellow-mortals. His message leaves us cold; it is his ardour which kindles us.

In other words, Sir Henry Newbolt appears to have involved himself in the old mistake that it is the philosophy of philosophical poetry that moves us. What moves us is the poetry; and, though it is difficult to separate the poetry of a philosophical poet from the intellectual argument which gives it form, the fact that we can and do continually refuse the philosophy and accept the poetry points to the likelihood that the philosophy merely serves the same office in philosophical poetry as the plot or myth in other kinds. We give to the one as to the other 'that willing suspension of disbelief which constitutes poetic faith'; if the poet is great enough to create, by means of his philosophy or his story, a significant order in the chaos of human experience, we ask no more from the philosophy.

So much at least seems true of the philosophic poetry of the past. Whether philosophic poetry is likely to be written in the future depends, therefore, upon the possibility of a metaphysical theory giving to the intellectual and emotional nature of a poet a satisfaction comparable with that given to Lucretius by the theory of Epicurus, or Dante by Thomism. And that, I think, is improbable.

In considering the question, we have to take into serious consideration the fact that we have no real philosophic poetry in English. Sometimes, it is true, Shelley is called a philosophical poet, sometimes Wordsworth; but in both cases by a manifest indulgence.

Of the process of intellectual argument they contain nothing: each, indeed, possessed a certain metaphysical faith, but, from the point of view of the logician, it was irrationally held. Shelley's Platonism was certainly not the outcome of Plato's dialectic; and Wordsworth's Pantheism was the product of immediate experience. They are philosophical only in the vaguest sense of the word, and it would be much nearer the mark to call them simply religious, as probably they would have been called had not orthodoxy in their day possessed a monopoly of the epithet.

Of Coleridge, on the other hand, it might fairly be said that he did possess the capacity to write a true philosophic poem: he could think severely and sustainedly, and, what is of no less consequence, the processes of his own abstract thought were attended by real emotional responses. To his intellectual dialectic there was, so to speak, a constant emotional corollary. Yet, strikingly enough, he made no attempt at the philosophic poem which he so much desired to be written, and seemed so abundantly qualified to write; he contented himself with urging the much less appropriately gifted Wordsworth to the task. Why did he thus draw back? It is not enough to whisper the word 'laudanum': only a few of the problems of Coleridge are explained by that easy word. It is more relevant to make clear to ourselves what Coleridge meant by 'a philosophical poem'. In a remarkable letter to Wordsworth he expounded his idea of what such a poem should be.

'I supposed you first to have meditated the faculties of man in the abstract, in their correspondence with his sphere of action, and first in feeling, touch, and taste, then in the eye, and last in the ear,—to have laid a solid and immovable foundation for the edifice by removing the sandy sophisms of Locke, and the mechanic dogmatists, and demonstrating that the senses were living growths and developments of the mind and spirit, in a much juster as well as higher sense, than the mind can be said to be formed by the senses. Next I understood that you would take the human race in the concrete, have exploded the absurd notion of Pope's *Essay on Man*, Darwin and all the countless believers even (strange to say) among Christians of man's having progressed from an ourang-outang state—so contrary to all history, to all religion, nay to all possibility—to have affirmed a Fall in some sense, as a fact, the possibility of which cannot be understood from the nature of the will, but the reality of which is attested by experience and conscience. Fallen men contemplated in the different ages of the world, and in the different states—savage, barbarous, civilized, the lonely cot or borderer's wigwam, the village, the manufacturing town, seaport, city, universities, and, not disguising the sore evils under which the whole creation groans, to point out, however, a manifest scheme of redemption, of reconciliation with this enmity with Nature—what are the obstacles, the *Antichrist* that must be and already is—and to conclude by a grand didactic swell on the necessary identity of a true philosophy with a true religion, agreeing in the results and differing only as the analytic and synthetic process, as discursive from intuitive, the former chiefly useful in perfecting the latter; in short the necessity for a general evolution in the modes of developing and disciplining the human mind by the substitution of life and intelligence (considered in its different powers from the plant up to that state in which the difference of degree becomes a new kind [man, self-consciousness], but yet not by essential opposition) for the philosophy of mechanism which, in everything that is most worthy of the human intellect, strikes *Death*, and cheats itself by mistaking clear images for distinct conceptions, and which idly demands conceptions where intuitions alone are possible or adequate to the majesty of Truth. In short, facts elevated into theory—

theory into laws—and laws into living and intelligent powers—true idealism necessarily perfecting itself in realism, realism refining itself into idealism.'

If we set aside the initial 'demonstration' of the absurdity of the sensationalist psychology which Coleridge demands, we see that the rest of the contemplated poem deals with man 'in the concrete'. The philosophical phases are simple. First, a Fall 'in some sense' would be affirmed on the evidence of experience and conscience; second, the way would be pointed to 'a manifest scheme of redemption', which, significantly, is equivalent to 'a reconciliation with this enmity with Nature'; and third, nothing less than a revolution in philosophy itself is to be proclaimed—'intuitions alone are adequate to the majesty of Truth'.

In order fully to grasp Coleridge's intention we need the aid of other passages in his writings. His conception of the 'Fall in some sense' is illuminated by his words in an appendix to 'Lay Sermons'. 'The soul, regarding Nature, seems to say to herself: "From this state hast *thou* fallen! Such shouldst thou still become, thyself all permeable to a higher power".' And again, 'What the plant is—by an act not its own and unconsciously, that thou must make thyself to become'. The 'manifest scheme of redemption' thus consists in the conscious achievement of a condition of pure spontaneity, in which state man should be so completely obedient to and expressive of Life as the rest of organic Nature appears to be. We may suppose that this belief, which recalls certain of the authentic sayings of Jesus, was reached by experience and intuition, and that it is itself an example of that superiority of intuition to conception which the whole poem was to establish. This process of intuition applied to living nature is what

Coleridge calls 'Reason', and, like Goethe, resolutely distinguishes from understanding. Indeed, Goethe's words to Eckermann provide the aptest commentary on Coleridge's thought:

'The Godhead is effective in the living and not in the dead, in the becoming and changing, not in the become and set-fast; and, therefore, similarly, the Reason is concerned only to strive towards the divine through the becoming and the living, and the Understanding only to make use of the become and the set-fast.'

Finally, with the identification of realism and idealism with which Coleridge's letter closes, we may compare his conviction that Nature is 'a symbol of the ideas of reason established in the truth of things'; and that 'a symbol is consubstantial with the truth of which it is the conductor'. So, 'the language of Nature is a subordinate Logos, that was in the beginning, and was with the thing it represented, and was the thing it represented'.

Thus we may describe the theme of Coleridge's philosophic poem as the supersession of ratiocination, by intuition; of understanding, by reason. This process, achieved in the individual man, was redemption: by it man became one with Nature, for the spark of intuitive Reason is kindled in him by a contemplation of Nature. The conflict of emotion and thought within himself is resolved, and his consciousness becomes as it were organically whole. Thus reintegrated, consciousness has an immediate apprehension of Truth, which is not abstract or ideal, but concrete and real. Nature *is* the Truth; and as man, by the attainment of Reason in himself, is reconciled with Nature, so he himself becomes part of the Truth—'all permeable to a higher power'.

The doctrine may seem difficult, or at least difficult to distinguish from a sort of Rousseauism. With Rousseauism it has little in common, though it has affinities to Rousseau. But it is, certain nuances of terminology apart, almost exactly identical with Goethe's philosophy; it is again very intimately connected with Keats's quite independent thinking, as will be apparent to any one who studies, with the care which it demands, Keats's famous letter on 'the Vale of Soul-making'. But the point for immediate emphasis is that this philosophy of Coleridge's is, like the related philosophies of Goethe and Keats, the philosophy of a poet. That is not to say it is inferior to the philosophy of a philosopher—I myself am convinced of the contrary—but it is profoundly different. For the true poet, the man 'gifted with more than ordinary organic sensibility', starts with an ineradicable faith in intuition. The faith may be unconscious, and very often it is never brought into the full light of consciousness; but the faith is there. The poet cannot help believing in intuition: he has it. And he is a poet because he has it. But all these three men—Coleridge, Goethe, and Keats—possessed besides their native poetic gift very great intellectual power, by which they were enabled to make the workings of their own mind distinct to themselves and to contemplate the nature of that intuitive faculty which was their birthright. Essentially, their philosophies are a reasoned justification of their own poetic processes of mind. Abstract conceptual thinking seemed to them always a rather clumsy substitute for a finer means of attaining truth of which they had actual experience.

Inevitably there must, to the philosopher, appear to be something paradoxical, if not wholly intangible, in this philosophy of poets; and that is the reason why the thinking of these three great men (even of Goethe) has never received any serious attention from professional philosophers. To follow their arguments, a certain capacity for the sideways glance is required. For here are men who, though certainly not inferior to the average philosopher in the faculty of discursive thinking, possessed another gift besides, to which they attached infinitely more importance, and which had, and was bound to have, a very potent influence on their abstract thinking. Though capable of abstract thinking, they were unable to *believe* in it as an instrument for attaining truth, for the simple reason that the divorce between the abstract and the concrete from which discourse takes its rise was overcome by their own peculiar faculty of intuition. The distinction between universal and particular could never be to them a distinction of the real, but only a distinction—and to them in their highest moments an unnecessary one—imposed upon the real. For them the particular *was* the universal; the real *was* the ideal. The identification may be disconcerting to the philosopher; but he ought to reckon with the fact that there is a kind of mind, and a very powerful kind of mind, to which that identification is necessary and inevitable—the beginning and the end of thinking.

One may get a pretty clear glimpse of the process of poetic thinking by reading Goethe's account of his reconciliation with Schiller, who had been deeply influenced by Kantian idealism. The dispute between the two men—Did Goethe's drawing of a typical plant represent an 'idea' or an 'experience'?—touched the centre of the problem. The dispute, it is true, was a dispute between two poets; but in reality it was a dispute between the purest type of poetic mind, with a reasoned and justified awareness of its own peculiar powers, and one less pure. Schiller combined—and in this he was very like Shelley—an impulsive, but very genuine poetic fluency, with an acquired philosophy. There was a liaison of discordant elements: Goethe, on the contrary, was *totus, teres atque rotundus*. And probably it was Schiller he had in mind when he wrote:

'There is a great difference between a poet who seeks the particular for the sake of the universal and one who seeks the universal in the particular. The former method breeds Allegory, where the particular is used only as an example, an instance, of the universal; but the latter is the true method of poetry. It expresses a particular without a thought of or a reference to the universal. But whoever has a living grasp of this particular grasps the universal with it, knowing it either not at all, or only long afterwards.'

It reminds one, very distinctly, of the letter Keats wrote to Shelley in August 1820, in acknowledgement of a copy of *The Cenci*.

'There is only one part of it I can judge of—the poetry and dramatic effect, which by many spirits now-a-days is considered the Mammon. A modern work, it is said, must have a purpose, which may be the God. An artist must serve Mammon; he must have "self-concentration"—selfishness, perhaps. You, I am sure, will forgive me for sincerely remarking that you might curb your magnanimity and be more of an artist, and load every rift of your subject with ore.'

One further sentence from Goethe's letters to Schiller will make clear the relation of thought between the two statements. 'The non-poet, just as much as the poet, can be moved by a poetical idea, but he cannot transfer it *into an object*, he cannot express it with a claim to inevitability.' The power, the universality, of poetry lies in its concreteness. The true poet's unremitting insistence upon particularity, which seems to the uncomprehending eye the service of Mammon, is, to the discerning vision, his own peculiar and inimitable service to God, to 'that subordinate Logos' of Nature—to repeat Coleridge's characteristic phrase—'which was with the thing it represented and was the thing it represented'.

Of course, it is evident that the most abstract and apparently logical of these statements is largely metaphorical. When Goethe insists that the true poet expresses a particular, and that whoever grasps this particular grasps the universal also with it, he is not speaking of the same universals and particulars as the logician. The man who grasps the particular person delineated by a dramatic poet, or the particular emotion expressed by a lyrical poet, cannot be said in either case to comprehend a logical universal. Something other than a concept is grasped, and another faculty than conceptual thinking is at work. The universals of poetry are not concepts, nor have they conceptual equivalents; Goethe was perfectly clear about that. What he was really saying is that in the true poetic activity of mind the logical distinction between particulars and universals is ignored, because it is invalid for that activity of mind. In poetry, *qua* poetry, there are neither particulars or universals, abstracts or concretes.

That is to say that, in the very method of poetry, a metaphysic is implicit. This was the metaphysic which Coleridge wished Wordsworth to make explicit in his 'great philosophical poem', the scheme of which he outlined in his letter. Yet Wordsworth did not write it, and Coleridge himself made no attempt. What was the reason for the failure?

We must remember that Wordsworth did make a beginning, and that Coleridge was once enthusiastic over it. It was *The Prelude*. We may suppose then that

Coleridge believed this was the right way to begin, namely, with an account of 'the growth of the poet's mind'. The poet would then show how the faculty of poetic thought came to be what it was, and how intuition, unconsciously active from childhood, came consciously to claim for itself the supreme position in the poet's mind. This was possible: this to a considerable extent Wordsworth actually did. But what then? Was not something very like a paradox imminent?

For if the poet was indeed the person he claimed to be, who by his intuition apprehended the truth, manifest where alone it could be manifest, in the infinite particularity of the universe, why trouble to explain what must in the nature of the case be either self-evident or not evident at all? Why not simply pursue his own natural task of making poetry in which the universality of the particular, the ideality of the real, should be made plain to those capable of seeing? What indeed was the purpose of a specifically philosophic poem, seeing that all true poetry—all poetry written according to Goethe's 'true poetic method'—contained, implicit in itself, a philosophy superior to all others? And, finally, how could such a philosophical poem be written, seeing that this true philosophy, proceeding from particular to particular, to intuition from intuition, was, by hypothesis, incapable of being fully explained in anything but non-philosophical poetry? Whether or not Coleridge ever presented this difficulty to himself in direct connexion with his demand for a philosophical poem, that he recognized it clearly enough in other contexts is evident from the nature of his praise of Shakespeare, whom he holds up constantly and with unvarying conviction, and not in a figurative sense, as the supreme philosopher.

In fact, Coleridge's position, stated in the simplest terms, was that the purest poetry was the purest philosophy. He had infinite difficulty in stating this in an intelligible form, because by definition a philosophy which proceeds from intuition to intuition is incapable of being apprehended save by intuition; and he was moreover involved in the impossible task of trying to find a conceptual language for processes of mind which were not conceptual at all. For this reason he has been, naturally but quite unwarrantably, accused of confusing poetic with conceptual thought in his criticism. He knew perfectly well—no man better—the difference between intuitive and discursive thinking; but he was compelled by the nature of his attempt continually to have recourse to clumsy intellectual equivalents for his intuitive processes. Thus when he describes Shakespeare's method as 'the observation of a mind, which having formed a theory and a system upon its own nature, remarks all things that are examples of its truth, and, above all, enabling it to convey the truths of philosophy as mere effects derived from what we may call the outward watchings of life', the 'theory', the 'system', the 'philosophy' of which he speaks are not at all what the ordinary dialectician would understand by such words. Coleridge is trying to find utterance for a thought which haunted him. We might gather a dozen other efforts to declare it. One shall suffice. 'It was Shakespeare's prerogative to have the universal which is potentially in each particular, opened out to him, the *homo generalis*, not as an abstraction from observation of a variety of men, but as the substance capable of endless modifications.' The power which Coleridge is attributing to Shakespeare is precisely the same as that which Goethe also made frequent efforts to distinguish:

the *anschauliche Urteilskraft*, the *exakte sinnliche Phantasie*—the power precisely of seeing the universal in the particular, of penetrating by intuition and self-knowledge into the creative force which is, and is recognized in, its differentiations.

The same inherent difficulty of language which has led to Coleridge's thinking being dismissed as transcendental and mystical must inevitably have recurred in an avowedly philosophic poem. It would have been well enough if Coleridge's mind had been inflamed by an alien system of philosophy; but that was impossible. He was a poet, with the poetic experience: the only philosophy that could satisfy him was the philosophy which set poetry in the supreme position which, he was intellectually convinced, it rightly occupied. The only way to express that philosophy was to practise it, and the only way to practise it was to be simply a creative poet.

It may be said that Coleridge's failure was the failure of a particular man, and that we must not draw a general conclusion from it. The objection is only plausible if we are prepared to challenge the truth of Coleridge's thought upon the nature of poetry. This, I think, is only possible to those who do not understand it. Therefore Coleridge's failure, and Wordsworth's, is really prophetic of the failure of all serious philosophical poetry in future. The attempt will be possible only to a poet who is less a poet and less a philosopher than he ought to be: it is condemned beforehand to second-rateness. Philosophical poetry can never again be great with the greatness of Lucretius or Dante, because, whenever a poet appears with a comparable poetic gift and a comparable 'depth and energy of thought', his intellectual power will be applied, as the intellectual power of Coleridge and Goethe and Keats was applied, to the justification of his own specifically poetic processes of mind.

The essential condition of philosophical poetry is that the poet should believe that there is a faculty of mind superior to the poetic; that was possible for Dante, tremendous poet though he was: but since Shakespeare lived and wrote it is not possible. Shakespeare created a new order of values, independent of the great medieval Christian tradition, yet spiritual through and through: a system of values, so far as we can see, completely divorced from any faith in immortality or after-justice, compatible, indeed, with a real agnosticism, yet in the height and breadth of the word profoundly religious. This system of values—which seems to us to have been produced like a creation of nature—makes a deep and undiminished appeal to us: generation after generation of men have meditated upon it, only to discover that this system of values is not a system at all. It satisfies, yet it cannot be analysed. The order is there, but it is the inscrutable order of organic life. And this extraordinary thing was produced by the poetic spirit, working free and autonomous, by a poet who trusted, as no poet had done before, or has done since, his own poetic genius.

The poets who, since Shakespeare, have been capable of philosophic poetry have had Shakespeare before them to show them what philosophic poetry can be. Perhaps, without his works before them, Goethe and Coleridge and Keats might not have reached the conclusions and certainties they did reach. Certainly no poets have ever been deeper and more understanding students of Shakespeare than these; and it is impossible that any poet of real stature who comes after them should not see Shakespeare largely through their eyes, and approach him by the road which their genius opened. The poet who follows them has no choice: he must realize that there is a profounder truth in Shakespeare than is contained in any philosophy, and that the poet becomes a truly philosophical poet, not by taking philosophy for his subject-matter or his inspiration, but by becoming wholly that which he potentially is—a revealer of the real. To the degree to which he follows the true method of poetry, the problems of philosophy cease to exist for him.

What, then—to return to the first cause of these reflections—can the prospect of an intellectual reconciliation of the conceptions of Time and Eternity, from which Sir Henry Newbolt expects so much, offer to a poet for whom the particular is, in fact, the universal? The reconciliation will be meaningless to him, because the divorce has never taken place. The things of time, the real world, truly seen, are to the poet completely significant. There is nothing higher than complete significance. The conception of an eternity, or of an eternal reality, different from the temporal, springs only from the sense of a partial or mutilated significance in the actual.

It is precisely this sense, which may be natural to man, which the great poet overcomes within himself. He does not judge experience; he submits himself to it: and he finds that the reality which presented itself to his intellectual consciousness as imperfect is received in a quite different way by the totality of his being. By the impact of that seemingly imperfect reality upon him, something is created in himself which declares that it is perfect. He recognizes the inevitability and beauty of his own painful experience, and with the same act of recognition bows himself to the inevitability and beauty of the things that are. Time is not to him a discordant and corrupting element; it is but a word for an aspect of the secret force of life itself, for the effective Godhead, which, as Goethe said, is 'effective in the living and not in the dead'. Time is but the intellectual abstraction of that reality which he knows immediately in himself as life—the pulse of his being. To shrink from Time is to shrink from Life itself.[1]

That is not to say that poets have not given voice to the anguish of the temporal—many have—nor that the poets who have done so are not poets. The contention is that, in so far as they remain in that predicament, they are incomplete and partial poets, who, through some defect of power, cannot make their rightful inheritance their own. The sense of exile is not the mark of major, but of minor, poetry; its persistence betokens a failure in poetic energy, an impotence to realize, or to be loyal to, the poetic nature. It is true that the note is recurrent in much of the poetry that is most generally admired; but that is because this emotion of exile is itself the most widespread in human hearts. The poetry of dream, in ages such as ours at least, finds a more ready response than the poetry of reality. But a growing nature quickly tires of it; it has no substance; it cannot give a final satisfaction. And to suppose it will gain substance by embracing a recondite philosophical notion of the ultimate convergence of Time and Eternity is an illusion. The anguish of the temporal will not be assuaged either in the poet who feels and communicates it, or the readers who respond to it, by any shadowy promise that in the dim and distant future men will feel it no more. The demand which the human soul makes

[1] See note p. 201.

is for satisfaction here and now; men's eyes must *see* their salvation.

It is this visible salvation that great poetry does offer. It faces the real, it extenuates nothing, shrinks from nothing: it gives us life as it is. And we discover that we can desire nothing more perfect, for we can conceive nothing more perfect to desire. That seems miracle enough; yet that alone will not suffice. For when the influence of the great poet's alchemy has passed from us, a question remains. If that which is possesses this perfection, then why struggle to achieve a better condition? This doubt often eats at the hearts of those religious souls who are in some degree responsive to the achievements of great poetry. It is the cause of that frequent revulsion in those who ponder the idea rather than experience the attitude of mind which often is called Pantheism. The great poet, no doubt, is a Pantheist; but he is primarily a poet. The Pantheism, which held as an intellectual creed might engender a Stoic resignation, is, as a poetic reality, a thing of potency—a *sursum corda*. For the poet's revelation of the perfection of what is kindles in our souls the desire to be able, with unaided vision, to see the perfection for ourselves. That is not easy: it calls for long and unrelenting effort, and for the power to accomplish in ourselves as much as in us lies of that patient submission to experience which the poet himself has practised. We at any rate, in order to behold the changeless beauty of the changing world, must ourselves be changed.

[FEBRUARY 1928

V

THE POETS' POET

A NEW and scholarly edition of Spenser has long been desired; and, since the publication of his masterly essay on the poet,[1] Professor Renwick was plainly indicated as the editor. The two volumes which have now appeared fulfil our expectations. The commentary of the editor is precisely the kind of commentary that is required. It indicates more thoroughly than has been done before the sources of Spenser's manifold and systematic borrowings. If, as is possible, a commentary of this kind seems to some laborious and even pedantic, it will be chiefly because they do not understand what manner of poet Spenser was; and if this judgement should seem to conflict with the judgement of Charles Lamb that Spenser is the poets' poet, that in its turn will be chiefly because the real implications of Lamb's words are not appreciated. For Lamb was not merely stating the simple fact that most of the English poets since Spenser's time have been deeply read in his work; he was also asserting that there was a very good reason why Spenser has always been beloved of his similars.

But since what was simple fact in Charles Lamb's day is simple fact no longer, we may refresh our memories. When Wordsworth heard, with his mind's ear, old Triton blow his wreathèd horn, the sound came to him through Spenser; when Keats sat down to write a new 'romance' and began—

Fair Isabel, poor simple Isabel . . .

[1] THE COMPLETE WORKS OF EDMUND SPENSER. Edited by *W. L. Renwick*. (The Scholartis Press.)

he was, whether he remembered it or not, singing over again a tune he had learned from Spenser—

> To Philemon, false faytour Philemon.

Again, even the very terms of that advice of Keats to Shelley, which some have found so harsh, that 'an artist must serve Mammon . . .' were derived from Spenser; nor can they be properly understood without a memory of the Cave of Mammon similar to that upon which Keats himself, consciously or unconsciously, was drawing. 'You will forgive me,' he said to Shelley, 'for sincerely remarking that you might curb your magnanimity, . . . and load every rift of your subject with ore.' What was in his mind was the house of Mammon.

> That house's forme within was rude and strong,
> Like an huge cave hewne out of rocky clifte,
> From whose rough vaut the ragged breaches hong
> Embost with massy gold of glorious guifte
> And with rich metall loaded every rifte. . . .

Keats's mind, indeed, was saturated with Spenser, whose influence upon him was second only to the more subtle and more intimate, and in a sense less scrutable, influence of Shakespeare. From Spenser, one might say, he learned to be a poet; from Shakespeare to be a great one.

Assuredly in Lamb's day Spenser was the poets' poet, as he had been Milton's poet, and probably at one time Shakespeare's also. But to-day things are different. True, Charles Doughty could proclaim 'Edmund, my lodestar'; but Doughty was writing an epic of England, in twenty-four books, and who can pay attention to-day to an epic in twenty-four books? Obviously, the same sort of people who can read *The Faerie Queene*—antediluvians manifest. For Spenser is, for the practical purposes of modern poetry, sadly out of fashion. And this is not because he is ancient simply; for one of the most resolutely modern of our poets can recommend his contemporary poets to seek in Dante their sustenance and the pattern of their skill. But Spenser belongs to the archaeology of literature.

This is strange, and worth consideration; for the tradition of English poetry is rooted in Spenser. And it is a very real question whether, if these roots are severed, English poetry will flourish again. Charles Doughty thought not. It is a pity that he never argued his opinion; he was content to assert it in the text of his epic from time to time, and get on with the writing. But, if he had argued it, he would have argued it, we may suppose, something in this fashion. Spenser, he would have said, is the great 'maker' of English poetry; he is the man who, by his learning, his passion, his exquisite sense of form and his delicate ear, was able to establish in the English tongue all that the English language would admit of the tunes and technique accumulated during the fifteen hundred years that European poetry had been extant. This was Spenser's service, done to English poetry, once for all; for what Spenser did not transmit to his poetic successors was not transmissible. It was not, so to say, poetic 'material'; it was idiosyncrasy, the ungovernable, incalculable and inimitable personal element—that which a poet cannot learn, but can only learn how to express. This fundamental distinction, between poetic commonplace and poetic idiosyncrasy, between impersonal and personal style, is itself alien to modern criticism. Whether it calls itself classical or romantic, modern criticism is on this essential point altogether romantic. It unquestioningly accepts the principle that 'le style, c'est l'homme même'; and almost as unquestioningly it accepts the converse of the dictum, 'l'homme même, c'est le style'. But the English romantics themselves, from whom this opinion ostensibly is derived, were not at all of this mind. They were conscious that their art was inherited; they conceived it as an acquisition, and they practised to acquire it. In their own view—surely a true one—they were not men who broke with the poetical tradition, but men who reasserted it. Since they were fine critics—indeed, their whole effort, like Spenser's own, was grounded on a deliberate critical realization—they distinguished, without difficulty, between the personal and the impersonal elements in the style of their great predecessors. For the impersonal element, which they might reasonably hope to acquire, they went chiefly to Spenser.

The reason why their example was not followed in the nineteenth century was partly, no doubt, because their practice was not understood; partly, also, because it was the inimitable, even the accidental, elements in their achievement which chiefly fascinated their successors. How great a mass of mid-nineteenth-century poetry and art, for instance, grew out of a single casual poem by Keats which he did not think worthy to be included in his last volume: *La Belle Dame sans Merci!* But certainly more important than either of these causes was the change that was taking place in the structure of English society. Democracy was establishing itself, and with democracy the democratic art of literature—the Novel. Whatever optimists may believe poetry is not a democratic art: it has never been, and never will be, unless the day shall arrive when democracy becomes itself aristocracy. It is futile to appeal to the example of the Ballads, which, however beautiful, do not at all belong to the kind of great poetry: or to the example of Shakespeare, whose *Hamlet* succeeded rather because it contained twenty-seven good pieces of stage-business than by reason of the poetry which Shakespeare could not keep out of it. The truth is that Keats himself was probably the last relatively poor man in England who was able honestly to believe that he might make a living by serving a full apprenticeship to the art of poetry. When at the beginning of *Endymion* he sat down to write to Haydon, quoting Spenser again,

> The noble hart that harbours vertuous thought,
> And is with childe of glorious great intent,
> Can never rest, untill it forth have brought
> Th' eternall brood of glorie excellent . . .

he really believed that by bringing forth that brood in the form of poetry he could achieve livelihood and fame. Nor was it an unreasonable illusion. His friends, some of them well-tried journalists, believed it. Yet more, his publisher believed it. Mr. Abbey, tea merchant and guardian, did not. Mr. Abbey was right.

There were popular poets in Keats's time: there was Scott, there was Byron, there was Moore. Whatever qualities they had, they had not the qualities of great poets. Thinking of them in 1864, Walter Bagehot wrote:

'Almost the sole result of the poetry of that time is the harm which it has done. It degraded for a time the whole character of the art. It fixed upon the minds of a whole generation, it engraved in popular memory and tradition, a vague conviction that poetry is but one of the many *amusements* for the enjoying classes, for the lighter hours of all classes. The mere notion, the bare idea, that poetry is a deep thing, a teaching thing, the most surely and wisely elevating of human things, is even now to the coarse public mind nearly unknown.'

Bagehot was expecting a change; but what was true of England in 1864 is equally true of England to-day. Our poetry is slight, occasional, indisputably minor. Only by thus circumscribing its intentions does it exist at all. The 'mere notion, the bare idea' that a man should, from the beginning, devote his life to poetry, to expressing through the medium of poetry the thought that is born of a lifetime's full experience, is become almost fantastic.

The position of Spenser, the great teacher of English poets, is therefore now anomalous. There is nobody for him to teach. All that he has to teach is precisely all that which is most irrelevant to the pursuit of literature to-day—the veritable 'art' of poetry, the specific skill by which a poet is a poet and not something else. Whether that situation is in itself deplorable or not, the consequence of the situation, with which we are here concerned, is a simple one—namely, that Spenser is not appreciated for the qualities that are peculiarly his own. He is judged, if judged at all, by standards which are not really germane to his intentions or his achievement; he is required to stand or fall by his intrinsic interestingness.

To require this of Spenser is unreasonable. But what seems unreasonable, to-day, is the assertion that the work of a great poet should be absolved from the application of a standard so obviously natural. If Spenser fails to interest, he fails in everything. But interestingness is relative. The criterion of interestingness which prevails under democratic conditions is that described by Dr. Johnson: 'Nothing can please many and please long but just representations of human nature.' It is, no doubt, the most essential kind of interestingness. Chaucer and Shakespeare both possess it in abundance; Spenser scarcely at all. But Spenser, though he aimed at pleasing long, did not aim at pleasing many. He was not even very much concerned with his own subject-matter, or at any rate he was concerned with it in a manner quite different from that in which he professed to be concerned with it. Its intrinsic interest for him, we may be sure, was very small. Provided that it was a subject-matter appropriate (by traditional canons) to a great poem, he was content. His aim was to write a great poem in the English language; it could be *about*—anything that great poems were about.

Much is sometimes made of Spenser's moral intention in composing *The Faerie Queene*; and, indeed, Spenser rather paraded it himself. But in reality this moral intention amounts to little. We have only to read, with an advised ear, the passage of most sustained and various beauty in *The Faerie Queene*—the adventure of Sir Guyon in the Gardens of Acrasia—to be certain that Spenser's heart was not in his morality. When, as in this episode, it came to a struggle between his morality and his sense of beauty, the sense of beauty, very properly, triumphed. The sense of beauty did with Spenser precisely what it did with his pupil Keats, 'it obliterated all consideration'. Spenser as a philosopher was hopelessly inconsistent, as a moralist hopelessly divided. He was fairly caught between the old ascetic morality and the new enthusiasm for Beauty for its own sake. He did not know whether Beauty was from God or the Devil; but it would not be true to say of him (as it would be true to say it of Marlowe or Shakespeare) that he did not care: he was, in this respect, a divided man. There was that in him which cared, and there was that in him—call it, with Coleridge, the genius in the man of genius—which did not care. This half-conscious, instinctive or intuitive part of him was content to suffer the sense of beauty to 'obliterate all consideration'. This was his destiny and he must follow it, even when it played havoc with his allegory and his conscious morality. Essentially, he was in much the same case as Keats when he wrote *Endymion*, inwardly impelled to trust to his sense of beauty, yet with his consciousness mistrusting his own faith, ostensibly even disowning it. Keats did not do this; but Spenser was near to the Middle Ages and Keats was far away. Keats was committed to find an individual solution for an individual problem, where Spenser could still, in consciousness at least, support himself with authority. Besides, Keats had time to think, where Spenser had not. The business in hand was too tremendous, too urgent, and too exciting to allow him to be turmoiled with its implications. The business in hand was making a great poem and laying the foundations of English poetry.

That English poetry should be beautiful, subtle, and inexhaustibly capable: that the instrument should henceforward have the capacity of 'divine respondence meet': that the language and the forms of English verse should become sensitive like that fair almond tree on Selinus, by whose vision Marlowe was entranced—

> Like to an almond tree ymounted hye
> On top of greene Selinis all alone,
> With blossoms brave bedecked daintily;
> Whose tender locks do tremble every one
> At everie little breath that under heaven is blowne—

this was the aim after which Spenser laboured as no English poet has laboured, nor needed to labour, since. The instrument which he devised, and shaped, and inlaid and polished is still *the* instrument of English poetry. Strings were added, like the blank verse of

Shakespeare and Milton, or the rich stanza of Keats's odes; or strings were taken away to make the heroic couplet of Dryden or of Pope. But the *sermo communis* of English poetry was settled: the themes, the tunes, the immense liberty of absolute and intricate formality, were won. All the great poets of England have known by simple instinct to whom they must go to learn their craft.

And surely, for those who have ears to hear, the sheer patterning of Spenser's 'music' has never been surpassed. Take these few passages which follow hard upon one another:

> Her wanton palfrey all was overspred
> With tinsel trappings woven like a wave
> Whose bridle hung with golden bells and bosses brave . . .
>
> Ah, deare Sansjoy, next dearest to Sansfoy,
> Cause of my new griefe, cause of my new joy . . .

or this, to link one stanza with another:

> Then turning to his Lady, dead with feare her found.
> Her seeming dead he found with feigned feare . . .

or this whole stanza:

> One day, nigh wearie of the yrksome way,
> From her unhastie beast she did alight;
> And on the grasse her dainty limbs did lay
> In secrete shadow, far from all men's sight:
> From her fayre head her fillet she undight
> And layd her stole aside. Her angel's face,
> As the great eye of heaven, shyned bright,
> And made a sunshine in the shady place;
> Did never mortall eye behold such heavenly grace.

But to attempt to exhibit the infinitely various modulations of Spenser's verse is a fantastic enterprise. Do we seek the characteristic music of Pope's heroic couplet? Here it is:

> Flesh without blood, a person without spright,
> Wounds without hurt, a body without might,
> That could doe harme, yet could not harmèd bee,
> That could not die, yet seemd a mortall wight,
> That was most strong in most infirmitee.

or take these two single lines from neighbouring stanzas, and recollect what Keats made of them:

> What hevens? what altars? what enraged heats? . . .
> And precious odours fetched from far away . . .

or the subsequent history of these:

> Come then; come soone; come sweetest death to me
> And take away this long lent loathed light:
> Sharp be thy wounds, but sweet the medicines be
> That long captived souls from weary thraldom free.

or this, for its own perfect felicity:

> Withall she laughed, and she blushed withall,
> That blushing to her laughter gave more grace,
> And laughter to her blushing, as did fall.

or—to make an end of the endless—this single line:

> Deep in the bottom of an huge great rock . . .

Lost in our admiration of this unbounded store of riches, we can only say, in Spenser's own words of the painter of Leda and the swan, 'O wondrous skill and sweet wit of the man!'

By common consent there is one perfect poem of Spenser's—'one entire and perfect chrysolite'—the *Epithalamion.* The reason of its universally recognized appeal is not far to seek: it lies in that which is, for the reader of Spenser as a whole, the subtle but immediately felt difference between this and all his other work, save the Sixth Book of *The Faerie Queene*—the contained tremor of an intimately personal emotion. It is but natural that those who have been rapt by the intoxication of this silver music should feel a faint sense of disappointment when they turn afterwards to his other work. But, rightly regarded, the *Epithalamion* is not an introduction to, but a culmination of, Spenser's poetry; it is the accidental triumph which he might easily never have had, but which none but himself could have won. Twenty-five years of toil at the sheer craft of poetry went to make that love-poem. And how many times in the history of a nation's literature does it happen that a mature and perfect poetic craftsman falls in love? Great poets have fallen in love often enough, and often enough have become great poets in part through that experience; but Spenser was complete when the experience came to him. If he himself was disturbed, his poetry could not be; it was immune from perturbation, for it was an impersonal thing.

Impersonal, in the strictest sense, no form of art can be; but the difference is immense between a form of art which is sustained by a pure aesthetic emotion and one which is primarily the expression of ordinary emotional and intellectual experience. The object in the one case is the making of a beautiful thing, in the other the communication of experience. No doubt these two distinct aims have been variously mingled in various poets, and in the same poet at various times; but in no English poet has the former aim been so completely dominant as in Spenser. He appears deliberately to have sacrificed to his ideal of formal poetic beauty a genuine personal emotion, even when the influence of that personal emotion was relevant and appropriate and even necessary. We have no reason to doubt that his grief over Sidney's death was sincere; *Astrophel*, nevertheless, is completely frigid. Matthew Roydon's companion elegy is simple and affecting beside it. And as this apparently deliberate sacrifice of personal emotion may be explained by the excessive strength of Spenser's passion for formal beauty, so the excessive strength of the passion itself may be explained by the evident difficulty which Spenser found in controlling his patterns. The lack of balance and proportion in a poem relatively so personal as *Colin Clout's Come Home Again* is very notable; so it is in *The Ruines of Time*. One feels that Spenser had always to keep a tight rein on himself, and that the apparent ease of his formal patterning was achieved only by a rigorous concentration.

We might put it that he could afford to run no risks by entertaining other emotions than those aroused by the pure pursuit of form and formal beauty. In such a statement there is inevitable exaggeration. But it is remarkable that both the morality and the imagery of *The Faerie Queene* are largely formal. In another, and perhaps a greater, kind of poet precisely these two elements are impassioned; his morality is what he intimately is, and his imagery is subdued to the urgency of his utterance. But in Spenser the morality is a mere convenience, or a useful theme, and the imagery quite often mere decorative fantasy. The meetings of a lion and a unicorn, or a gryphon and a dragon, provide poor similes: they are there not from any inherent necessity, but because images are formally required. It is only when he leaves for the time being the company of his patterns of virtue and comes nearer to the actual world of men that his imagery is more than abstract decoration. And in this regard one can mark a sort of progress towards reality. When Paridel has cast off Hellenore,

Alone he rode without his Paragone;
For, having filcht her bells, her up he cast
To the wide world, and left her fly alone:
He nould be clogd. So had he served many one,

when Trompart lays his snare for Malbecco,

Yet stoupt he not, but lay still in the winde,
Waiting advantage on his pray to sease . . .

the images do more than decorate, they define; and by the time we have reached the pastoral loveliness of the Sixth Book we are scarcely surprised by the simple perfection of what is surely the most dramatically appropriate image in all Spenser, when Calidore makes the enchanting Tristram his squire:

So he him dubbed, and his Squire did call.
Full glad and joyous then young Tristram grew;
Like as a flowre, whose silken leaves small
Long shut up in the bud from heavens vew,
At length breakes forth, and brode displays his smyling hew.

The Sixth Book is perhaps no more truly characteristic of Spenser than the *Epithalamion*, with which it is probably contemporary; into both alike enters a warm fragrance of reality. In Calidore morality steps down from the abstract empyrean and is incarnate and humane, wayward and lovely. In Calidore, as in young Tristram, it veritably flowers. And being humane, it does not even pretend to stifle in itself the lust of the eye and the pride of life. No whisper of conscience, nor monition of Palmer, warns Calidore that he is on the road to damnation when he peeps from the covert of the wood:

There did he see that pleased much his sight
That even he him selfe his eies envyde,
An hundred naked maidens lilly white
All raunged in a ring and dauncing in delight.

And since Colin Clout ('who knows not Colin Clout?') was in the midst of them, piping so merrily as never none, it is clear that Calidore was not in temptation, but in Elysium. It is woefully inconsistent with all that had gone before. Poor harried Acrasia and her lovely maidens, in sober justice, should have burst like a troop of Maenads into that naked conclave, for revenge. But the writ of sober justice does not run in the world of imagination. Colin Clout had no need to be abashed by the invasion; he had only to trust his genius and let it speak for him. 'It was I,' his genius would have said to Acrasia and her maidens, 'who called you out of nothingness and made you lovely; it was not I who destroyed you. For I am Imagination, who, having once created beauty, can never destroy it again. Join in the dance.' And the enchantment of the Sixth Book is that we feel that Acrasia and her maidens have joined in the dance, in virtue of that title which Keats proclaimed: 'What the Imagination seizes as Beauty must be Truth.'

It is an old problem, this of Art and Morality, solved in fact easily enough by those who have the strength to make either a morality of their art or an art of their morality, but a cause of incessant perplexity to those without the courage to do either. Spenser, we know, did the former; and few who read him well will not be inwardly convinced that he did the latter also. The poet who conceived his ideal in the semblance of Sir Calidore, it is true, may not himself have been much like him; and perhaps that perfection of grace in conduct was no more the gift of the gods to Spenser than the perfection of grace in his poetry. After all, he half-confesses as much when he speaks of Sir Calidore's courtesy:

Thereto great help Dame Nature selfe doth lend;
For some so goodly gratious are by kind,
That every action doth them much commend
And in the eyes of men great liking find;
Which others that have greater skill in mind,
Though they enforce themselves, cannot attain;
For everie thing to which one is inclin'd
Doth best become and greatest grace doth gaine:
Yet praise likewise deserve good thewes enforst with paine.

'Good thewes enforst with paine'—that is certainly the chief secret of Spenser's great and enduring achievement in poetry; quite possibly it was also the cause of his long wooing of his wife.

But the long wooing had a happy ending; and something of Spenser's moment of felicity is suffused through the Sixth Book, as it is through the *Epithalamion*. The five books which precede it are romance; the sixth is simply romantic, in the sense in which *As You Like It* and *A Winter's Tale* are romantic. The characters are real, their virtue and their love both credible and charming. We enter into a different world which, if it is not the world of every day, is at least a world into which if the fates were propitious and the stars dancing, the world of every day might be transmuted. And the tense atmosphere of derring-do is so mightily relaxed in this happy kingdom that nobody cares, though Sir Calidore forgets all about his blatant enemy for long months on end. The air is kindly here; the salvage man discovers himself the pattern of courtesy, cruel ladies learn to be kind, and tyrannous husbands are taught to be gentle. *Redeunt Saturnia regna.*

[FEBRUARY 1930

VI

NORTH'S PLUTARCH

North's Plutarch shares with Florio's Montaigne the honour of being, after the English Bible, the most famous of the great Elizabethan translations. Between them they represent the best of which Elizabethan translation was capable. Perhaps there were more exact translations, but none were more significant than these. Through the one, all that was most assimilable in classical antiquity, through the other, all that was most valuable in the response of a sane and enlightened European mind to the enlargement of experience by classical antiquity, was communicated to the ordinary Elizabethan.

It would be pleasantly harmonious if we could point to evidences, equally indisputable in either case, of the influence of these two translations on the great exemplar of the ordinary Elizabethan—William Shakespeare. But, though it is quite possible that Shakespeare was influenced by Florio's Montaigne, it is evident that he made little practical use of it. There are, as critics have pointed out, affinities between the intellectual atmosphere of *Hamlet* and *An Apologie of Raymond Sebond*; but affinities of this kind may as well be due to the analogous development of kindred minds responsive to much the same experience. On such matters there is hardly even a subjective certainty to be had. In *An Apologie of Raymond Sebond* Montaigne writes:

'Philosophy hath indeed armed man for the enduring of all other accidents, whether with patience, or if it be over-costly to be found, with an infallible defeat in conveying herself altogether from the sense; but they are meanes which serve a soule that is her owne, and in her proper force capable of discourse and deliberation: not serving to this inconvenience where with a Philosopher, a soule becommeth the soule of a foole, troubled, vanquished, and lost. Which divers occasions may produce, as in an over-violent agitation, which by some vehement passion the soule may beget in her selfe: or a hurt in some part of the body, or an exhalation from the stomacke, casting us into some astonishment, dazling, or giddiness of the head. . . . Philosophers have, in mine opinion, but slightly harpt upon this string, no more than other of like consequence.'

Shakespeare, in *Much Ado*, sums up the argument wittily:

> For there was never yet philosopher
> That could endure the toothache patiently,
> However they have writ the style of gods
> And made a push at chance and sufferance.

But it would need a bold critic to maintain that Shakespeare learnt it from Montaigne. A shrewd and sceptical mind has not much difficulty in reaching such conclusions unaided.

What we might say, judging by Shakespeare's dealings with North's Plutarch, is that if Florio's Montaigne could have saved him trouble he would gladly have incorporated some of it in his work. Since it is almost impossible to imagine that he did not read Florio's Montaigne, the negative evidence suggests that Montaigne did not save him trouble. He could do Montaigne's thinking, perhaps too easily, for himself; and as for Montaigne's facts, they were either facts of Shakespeare's experience also, or he had most of them already in Plutarch. He could ponder on the antique world which Plutarch revealed as well as Montaigne himself. What effect it chiefly made on him would be a nice question. Perhaps, for the general award, he would have endorsed the verdict contained in the life of Plutarch which was added to the 1603 edition of North:

'For if ever there were booke, next to that we call the holy Scriptures, it may be said that that which containeth the lives of the noble GREEKES and ROMAINES is an assured testimonie of many hundreds of yeares, a Sunne of veritie, a life of memorie, a true mistresse of life, and an excellent messenger of antiquitie.'

That, at all events, was substantially the verdict of Europe; even Rousseau, in his *Émile*, a century and a half later, could only confirm it. But in the case of Shakespeare we should like something more particular. And perhaps we can guess at it. He had his sceptical moments—Falstaff might 'justly say, with the hook-nosed fellow of Rome: I came, saw, and overcame', and once there is ominous talk of 'playing the Roman fool' —but in the main he was deeply and durably impressed with the majesty of Rome. Ben Jonson, whose knowledge of classical antiquity was more exact, but not necessarily more true, found fault with Shakespeare for writing

Caesar did never wrong but with just cause.

And it is probable that Shakespeare, in response to Jonson's ridicule, altered the line to what we have. But there is that in Shakespeare's original line which springs from and expresses a true historical imagination. That it was no mere rhetorical hyperbole of Shakespeare's is evident from the quality of his response to Roman grandeur. 'I am more an antique Roman than a Dane', cries Horatio, preparing to follow Hamlet across the bourn from which no traveller returns; and Cleopatra proclaims a like resolve more thrillingly still:

And then, what's brave, what's noble,

Let 's do it after the high Roman fashion,
And make death proud to take us.

Through Plutarch he saw an heroic Rome: a mode of life wherein some chosen men seemed to stand for a moment co-equal with Destiny—a giant world. In *Julius Caesar* the effect is described, but hardly realized:

Why, man, he doth bestride the narrow world
Like a Colossus; and we petty men
Walk under his huge legs and peep about
To find ourselves dishonourable graves.

The Caesar he sets before us, as many critics in one form or another, have pointed out, is not such a Caesar: he is a mortal man with the falling sickness, who yields in actual and objective majesty to the two conspirators. But it would be rash to conclude from this that Shakespeare was lacking in sympathy with Caesar, though sympathy would never be the right word for what Shakespeare felt about him. It is far more likely that Shakespeare, when he wrote his play, simply did not know how to deal with the mightiest figure of antique Rome. And North's Plutarch did not help him. For Plutarch himself is unresponsive to Caesar. As he depicts him, Caesar is a shadowy figure who, by some mechanical miracle, achieves amazing results. His victories are a prodigious list, but only a list. Pompey, with his contradictions, Crassus, with his tragedy, Sertorius, with his romance—these are heroes to Plutarch; to Caesar he grudges everything. He is, almost deliberately, unjust to him: he speaks of Caesar as solely responsible for the downfall of Rome, though he must have known perfectly well—indeed, in one place he admits it—that Marius and Sulla, Pompey and Crassus, sought no different end from Caesar. But they in some way fell short where Caesar succeeded; and Caesar must suffer for it. It was not the sense that failure makes for tragic grandeur which made Plutarch so niggardly to Caesar—Sulla was no failure; it was what the Germans have called the 'petty-state' (*kleinstädtisch*) mentality. In Plutarch it had more excuse than in Germany: he inherited the tradition of the Greek city-state of which Caesar and Caesarism marked the final end.

That Shakespeare could not penetrate beyond Plutarch's biased and grudging picture we may, if we will, put down to a deficiency in him. But historical realism was very slow in coming; and we must suppose that, with his small Latin, Shakespeare had little else than Plutarch to go upon. But the nature of Shakespeare's dependence upon North is revealed even more clearly by the quality of his response when Plutarch gave him a real opening. The life of Antonius is the most opulently coloured of all Plutarch's lives; it is richer, even, than the life of Alexander. And this, it seems, for oddly mixed reasons. There is a great woman in the story: a living and most queenly queen. Whether there was, or was not, such another figure in history, there was certainly not such another in Plutarch's pages. Secondly, Plutarch's life of Antony glows with the colour of almost first-hand experience.

'I have heard my grandfather *Lampryas* report that one *Philotas* a phisition, borne in the citie of AMPHISSA, told him that he was at that present time in ALEXANDRIA, and studied Phisicke: and that having acquaintance with one of *Antonius* cookes, he tooke him with him to *Antonius* house, (being a young man desirous to see things) to shew him the wonderfull sumptuous charge and preparation of one only supper. When he was in the kitchin, and saw a world of diversities of meates, and amongst others, eight wild boares rosted whole: he began to wonder at it, and sayd, sure you have a great number of ghests to supper. The cooke fell a laughing, and answered him, no (quod he) not many ghestes, nor above twelve in all: but yet all that is boyled or rosted must be served in whole, or else it would be marred straight. For *Antonius* peradventure will suppe presently, or it may be a pretie while hence, or likely enough he will deferre it longer, for that he hath dranke well to day, or else hath had some other great matters in hand: and therefore we doe not dresse one supper only, but many suppers, bicause we are uncerteine of the houre he will suppe in. *Philotas* the Phisition tolde my grandfather this tale. . . .'

Those eight wild boars to twelve persons are in Shakespeare's *Antony.* Likewise the other grandfather of Plutarch, Nicarchus, told the story how all the citizens of Chaeronea ('not one excepted') were made to carry corn down to the sea for Antony's fleet: and helped along with whips. But when they loaded up for the second journey, 'news came that Antonius had lost the battel, and so escaped our poor citie'.

No other of Plutarch's lives has such touches. They not merely remind us that to the Greek world Antony, above all other Romans, was an intimate reality, and that his fatal dalliance with Cleopatra was, for a Greek, a supreme example of the magic by which conquered Greece led captive its fierce conquerors; they also suggest that much of the sheer magnificence of Shakespeare's play is directly due to the distant accident that brought Antony closer than his Roman similars to the Greek world and the Greek mind. For it seems to one who compares the life of Antonius with the other lives in North from which Shakespeare drew his Roman plays, and compares these plays also among themselves, that, as in *Julius Caesar* and *Coriolanus*, so in *Antony and Cleopatra*,

Shakespeare merely intensified the qualities of his original. Such 'mere intensification' is, of course, a relative phrase; but it is used to imply that the peculiar opulence of *Antony and Cleopatra* comes as much from the subject as from the author: is North's no less than Shakespeare's. This unparalleled magnificence has never been better or more briefly conveyed than by Keats in a letter to Haydon:

> 'When a Schoolboy the abstract Idea I had of an heroic painting—was what I cannot describe. I saw it somewhat sideways, large, prominent, round, and colour'd with magnificence—somewhat like the feel I have of Antony and Cleopatra. Or of Alcibiades leaning on his Crimson Couch in his Galley, his broad shoulders imperceptibly heaving with the Sea.'

But precisely that kind of opulence is in Plutarch also. Every one knows that the famous picture of Cleopatra's meeting with Antony ('The barge she sat in like a burnished throne, Burn'd on the water . . .') comes, with the addition of four magical images, bodily from North. Not so many are aware of the peculiar richness of detail in Plutarch's story compared with his other lives. North's Plutarch is not all like that, nor nearly all. We have to read a great many lives before we find (perhaps in the life of Alexander) a physical picture of the hero such as Plutarch gives of Antony.

> 'He had a noble presence, and shewed a countenaunce of one of a noble house: he had a goodly thicke beard, a broad forehead, crooke nosed, and there appeared such a manly looke in his countenaunce, as is commonly seene in *Hercules* pictures, stamped or graven in mettell.'

And we should have to look still farther (to the life of Pyrrhus, where we are told of Alexander's 'high voice') for such another description of a hero's actual manner of speech as Plutarch provides for Antony.

'He used a manner of phrase in his speeche called Asiatik, which caried the best grace and estimation at that time, and was much like to his manners and life: for it was full of ostentation, foolishe braverie, and vaine ambition.'

There, probably, speaks the Greek trained in the Attic school. But what a hint for the poet capable of taking it!

That the original and the theme had more to do with the peculiar luxuriance of Shakespeare's play than any independent development of his own is shown by the striking spareness of *Coriolanus*, which is almost contemporary with *Antony and Cleopatra*. The versification in both belongs to the same period; it is Shakespeare's maturest and least imitable. It is pure munificence of decoration that separates them as art—the evident determination of Shakespeare in writing *Antony and Cleopatra* to 'load every rift with ore', in much the same way as Keats himself loaded every rift with ore when he wrote *The Eve of St. Agnes*. There was no escape, even if we can imagine that Shakespeare had any desire to escape. The model was before him. Plutarch's story, as rendered by North, is magnificent and vivid in a certain definite way. Shakespeare had no choice, if he was to deal with the theme at all; he had to be more magnificent, and more vivid, in the same definite way. And he was.

Here, too, we have an explanation of the kaleidoscopic shifting of scene which is so often objected against *Antony and Cleopatra*. Shakespeare could not avoid it, if he was to surpass his original. It might be argued that if he had been more of an artist he would not even have attempted this simple transposition of North's story—the analogue of a film-scenario—but would have set himself to convert it utterly into pure drama. How much of an 'artist' in the modern sense Shakespeare was will never be settled; but the chances are heavy that in this particular case he was deliberately neglectful of 'theatre'—even of Elizabethan 'theatre'. He had a chance to be pure poet, and he was independent enough to be able to take it with both hands. There was little indeed that could be left out. The first part of the story in North was covered by *Julius Caesar*. Of what remained practically nothing could be sacrificed without evident loss. When the manifest digressions were eliminated the rest was almost all pure gold. The raising of the dying Antony into the monument is really no more than a typical specimen.

They that were present to behold it, said they never saw so pitiefull a sight. For, they plucked up poore *Antonius* all bloody as he was, and drawing on with pangs of death, who holding up his hands to *Cleopatra*, raised up himself as well as he could. It was a hard thing for these women to do, to lift him up: but *Cleopatra* stowping downe with her head, putting to all her strength to her uttermost power did lift him up with much a doe, and never let go her hold, with the helpe of the women beneath that bad her be of corage, and were as sorie to see her labor so, as she her selfe. So when she had gotten him in after that sorte, and layed him on a bed: she rent her garments upon him, clapping her brest, and scratching her face and stomake. Then she dried up his blood that had berayed his face, and called him her Lord, her husband, and Emperor, forgetting her owne miserie and calamity, for the pitie and compassion she tooke of him. *Antonius* made her cease her lamenting, and called for wine, either bicause he was a thirst, or else for that he thought thereby to hasten his death. When he had dronke, he earnestly prayed her, and perswaded her, that she would seeke to save her own life, if she could possible, without reproche and dishonor: and that chiefly she should trust *Proculeius* above any man else about *Caesar*. And as for him selfe, that she should not lament nor sorrowe for the miserable chaunge of his fortune at the end of his dayes: but rather that she should thinke him the more fortunate, for the former triumphes and honors he had received, considering that while he lived he was the noblest and greatest Prince of the world, and that now he was overcome, not cowardly, but valiantly, a ROMANE by an other ROMANE.'

No narrative, it seems, could well be nobler. But it is heightened by Shakespeare. At the beginning of his transposition of this passage he puts unearthly music of the imagination in Cleopatra's lips.

> O sun,
> Burn the great sphere thou movest in! Darkling stand
> The varying shore of the world!

And at the end, some more:

> The crown o' the earth doth melt. My lord!
> O wither'd is the garland of the war,
> The soldier's pole is fall'n: young boys and girls
> Are level now with men; the odds is gone
> And there is nothing left remarkable
> Beneath the visiting moon.

With such an overture and finale the passage is set. Perhaps writing of that kind was easy for Shakespeare; perhaps it was easy for him to turn the speech of Antony into this:

> The miserable change now at my end
> Lament nor sorrow at; but please your thoughts
> In feeding them with those my former fortunes
> Wherein I lived, the greatest prince o' the world,
> The noblest; and do now not basely die,
> Not cowardly put off my helmet to
> My countryman—a Roman by a Roman
> Valiantly vanquished.

Probably it was very easy for him: for it looks as though more lines were written with a running pen with the text of North before him. But there was one passage at least on which he could work no heightening change at all. The real question was rather by how much he would fail.

'But when they had opened the dores they founde *Cleopatra* starke dead, layed upon a bed of gold, attired and araied in her royall robes, and one of her two women, which was called *Iras*, dead at her feete: and her other woman called *Charmion* halfe dead, and trembling, trimming the Diademe which *Cleopatra* ware upon her head. One of the souldiers seeing her, angrily sayd unto her: is that well done *Charmion*? Verie well sayd she againe, and meete for a Princes discended from the race of so many noble Kings. She sayd no more, but fell downe dead hard by the bed.'

Of that Shakespeare could give but little. But he made Charmian say 'It is well done'—surely the only perfection that it was possible to add, to compensate for those that poetry was bound to sacrifice.

To regard North's Plutarch as the raw material of some of Shakespeare's plays may seem inadequate appreciation. But there can be no doubt that Shakespeare's use of North is the book's supreme title to fame. Shakespeare treated no other book in this fashion; no other man's writing did he thus openly incorporate into his own. And in none of the three plays which he based on North did he use his original so steadily and completely as he did in *Antony and Cleopatra*. In other plays we might conceivably suspect him of saving time and trouble, but in this it is not possible. He used North's language because he had none better. A close and patient study of precisely what he used of North—not passages merely, but isolated words—is one of the most open and least doubtful roads we have into the workings of Shakespeare's mind. His handling of the life of Antonius is a miracle of discrimination.

For North is by no means always—by no means frequently even—a master. After all, in its day, North's Plutarch was journeyman work, as was Florio's Montaigne. It has not, and could not be expected to have, the sustained magnificence of the masterpiece of all Elizabethan translation—our English Bible. North, we can feel, went on and on; and quite often he went on and on and clean forgot the necessity (if it was a thing he ever consciously remembered) of pulling himself and his period together. But there was a great difference between going on and on in those days and going on and on in ours. Our translators go on and on along railway lines; North went on and on in a kind of exploration. He was exploring a language—our own. Sometimes the language will not respond to the demands that Amyot's French makes upon it; it shows naïve, ungainly, and coltish in idiom, or more often loose-jointed in syntax, and confused in *ordonnance*. But, on the whole, the staple is admirable. Consider the very different excellences of these three passages.

'For there is no exercise or occupation in the world, which so sodainely bringeth a man to love and desire quietnes, as doth husbandrie and tillage: and yet to defend a mans own, there is in it corage and hardiness to fight. But greedy desire, violently to take from others, and unjustely to occupie that is none of theirs, is never in right husbandmen.' (*Life of Numa.*)

It is hardly possible to be clearer, or more forcible, or more concise.

Or, again, his rendering of the story with which

Plutarch comments on the absence of any declared cause for Paulus Emilius's divorce of his wife.

'Me thinckes the tale that is tolde concerning the separation of a certaine marriage is true. That a certen ROMAINE having forsaken his wife, her friendes fell out with him, and asked him: what fault dost thou finde in her? is she not honest of her bodie? is she not fayer? doth she not bring thee goodly children? But he putting forth his foote, shewed them his shooe, and aunswered them. Is not this a goodly shooe? is it not finely made? and is not it newe? yet I dare saye there is never a one of you can tell where it wringeth me.'

Finally, in a matter more ambitious, which invites a more direct comparison with modern methods, this character of Sertorius:

'He was never greatly moved, with feare, nor joy; but as he was a resolute man without feare in most daunger, so was he most temperate in greatest prosperitie. In valiantnes inferior to no Captaine of his time, and very quicke of execution in every imminent daunger. For where any present exployt was to be done, any strong place of advantage to lodge or fight in to be taken, or that he was to passe over any river, or scape any instant daunger where it stoode upon speedy execution, and to show some stratageame or policie in time and place to supplant the enemie: in those matters he passingly excelled. Furthermore, he was both bountifull in rewarding good service, and mercifull in punishing of offenders; but this notwithstanding, the fowle murther he did in his latter days upon certaine younge children that were pledges with him (which doubtlesse was an act of great cruelty and anger that could not forgeve) doth manifestlie prove, that he was neither mercifull nor curteous of nature: but that he manie times did finely counterfeat it, when both the time and the warres did so require it. But for mine own opinion, sure I am perswaded that no misfortune can have power to make perfite virtue, grounded upon good reason, to worke in any sort contrarie to it selfe; neither doe I think it impossible also, but that men's good willes and gentle natures being injured without cause, may peradventure change their naturall dispositions. Which then proved true in *Sertorius*, who finding fortune contrary to him, and his good happe chaunging to ill, grewe so crabbed and fierce of nature, that he would take cruell revenge of them which had villanously betraied him.'

In that passage, excellent though it is, we have a glimpse of North's weakness; it is a weakness of Florio also, and of all the Elizabethan translators. Their psychological discrimination is fumbling. Instead of sharpening Amyot's language in this respect, North blurs it further. As North renders it, the passage is at bottom contradictory. Sertorius was not merciful by nature, but assumed the virtue; for no misfortune can alter true virtue. But men's natural dispositions to mercy may be changed by violence of fortune. And this was the case with Sertorius. That North fumbled over the word 'nature' is no great crime: it still confuses men. But it is obvious that his psychology is haphazard. He did not really know what he was supposed to be saying about Sertorius. Failures of this kind are fairly frequent in North. When the psychology becomes at all complex, he also becomes uncertain.

In their efforts to conquer these difficulties, which North sometimes failed to overcome, lay the greatest service of such translators to the language of English prose. They were making it adequate to the self-knowledge of civilized men. It seems strange to us that the verse of Shakespeare should have been so much more supple and responsive to the nuance of thought and emotion than the prose of his contemporaries; but when we reflect that only fifty years before Shakespeare's birth the prose language of humane knowledge was almost universally Latin, while there was some tradition of vernacular verse, it becomes less surprising. Possibly Shakespeare himself possessed a mastery in both kinds. But it is difficult to compare the prose of dramatic dialogue with the prose of description and argument. The only considerable specimen of this latter which we have from Shakespeare is his argument to *The Rape of Lucrece*. This is very good; for a young man truly excellent. What his prose in the same kind would have been ten or fifteen years later we can only conjecture. But it is certain that when he makes use of a piece of North's prose and turns it into his own verse it becomes not merely more concise but far clearer. The sequence of thought and emotion is made more distinct. A good instance of his method is his handling of Volumnia's speech to Coriolanus.

'If we helde our peace (my sonne) and determined not to speake, the state of our poore bodies, and present sight of our rayment, would easely bewray to thee what life we have led at home, since thy exile and abode abroad. But thinke now with thy selfe, howe much more unfortunatly, then all the women livinge we are come hether, considering that the sight which should be most pleasaunt to all other to beholde, spitefull fortune hath made most fearefull to us: making my selfe to see my sonne, and my daughter here, her husband, besieging the walls of his native countrie. So as that which is thonly comforte to all other in their adversitie and miserie, to pray unto the goddes, and to call them for aide: is the onely thing which plongeth us into most deepe perplexitie. For we can not (alas) together pray, both for victorie, for our countrie, and for the safetie of thy life also: but a worlde of grievous curses, yea more than any mortall enemie can heap uppon us, are forcibly wrapt up in our prayers. For the bitter soppe of most harde choyce is offered thy wife and children, to forgoe the one of the two; either to lose the person of thy selfe, or the nurse of their native countrie. For my selfe (my sonne) I am determined not to tarry, till fortune in my life time make an ende of this warre. For if I cannot persuade thee, rather to doe good unto both parties, then to overthrowe and destroye the one, preferring love and nature, before the malice and calamitie of wars: thou shalt see, my sonne, and trust unto it, thou shalt no sooner marche forward to assault thy countrie, but thy foote shall tread upon thy mother's womb, that brought thee first into this world. And I may not deferre to see the daye, either that my sonne be led prisoner to triumph by his naturall country men, or that he him selfe doe triumph of them, and of his natural countrie.'

What is most striking in Shakespeare's transposition of of th isspeech is the emotional rearrangement. A real concentration takes the place of an emotional diffusion.

> Should we be silent and not speak, our raiment
> And state of bodies would bewray what life
> We have led since thy exile. Think with thyself
> How more unfortunate than all living women
> Are we come hither: since that thy sight, which should
> Make our eyes flow with joy, hearts dance with comforts,
> Constrains them weep, and shake with fear and sorrow:
> Making the mother, wife, and child to see
> The son, the husband, and the father tearing
> His country's bowels out. And to poor we
> Thine enmity 's most capital: thou barr'st us
> Our prayers to the gods, which is a comfort
> That all but we enjoy; for how can we,
> Alas, how can we for our country pray,
> Whereto we are bound, together with thy victory,
> Whereto we are bound? Alack, or we must lose
> The country, our dear nurse, or else thy person,
> Our comfort in the country. We must find

An evident calamity, though we had
Our wish, which side should win: for either thou
Must, as a foreign recreant, be led
With manacles through our streets, or else
Triumphantly tread on thy country's ruin,
And bear the palm for having bravely shed
Thy wife and children's blood. For myself, son,
I purpose not to wait on fortune till
These wars determine: if I cannot persuade thee
Rather to show a noble grace to both parts
Than seek the end of one, thou shalt no sooner
March to assault thy country than to tread—
Trust to 't, thou shalt not—on thy mother's womb
That brought thee to this world.

What chiefly distinguishes this verse from North's prose is not specifically 'poetic' quality, but a very marked increase in clarity and *ordonnance*. The simple shifting of the position of North's last sentence is extraordinarily effective. But at every turn where North tends to slackness and obscurity, Shakespeare is crisp and clear. In only one place can we definitely say that his verse pattern directly aided him in this. The second 'How *can* we?'—bearing a different emphasis from the first—is an effect proper to the medium. But the clarity of: 'Alack, or we must lose the country, our dear nurse, or else thy person, our comfort in the country,' compared with North's corresponding sentence, is simply the clarity of a mind of superior energy.

Conceived ideally as a tacit criticism of North, Shakespeare's rewriting is illuminating. Leaving the question of genius aside, we cannot imagine any one writing English, in verse or prose, of the same strength and intensity in 1575, when North began to be busy with his rendering of Amyot. The language itself was incapable of it. Even the discipline of euphuism had scarcely begun. Just at the time that North had finished his Plutarch, Sidney was engaged in his *Arcadia*. That is a far less enjoyable book to read than North; but, as prose, it marks a perceptible advance. It is responsive to more of psychological subtlety. Compare North's confused description of the nature of Sertorius, with an apposite sentence from Sidney:

> 'It comes of a very ill grounde, that ignorance should be the mother of faithfullness. O, no, he cannot be good, that knows not why he is good, but stands so far good, as his fortune may keep him unassayed, but, coming to it, his rude simplicity is either easily changed, or easily deceived.'

The antithetical and balanced structure is not merely a decorative but a substantial refinement; it is an added capacity of expression. The enrichment, we can see, has been taken up into Shakespeare's verse. By his rearrangement he emphasizes the antitheses which are implicit in North's prose, and gives it at once a new complexity and a new clarity.

What intellectual structure North's prose possesses derives from its original. In the process of translation it is diminished, not increased. If we speak of his Plutarch as a masterpiece, therefore, we must be clear about what we mean. His plain narrative is for the most part admirable; his language is unstaled, he is troubled by no thoughts of decorum, no possibility of a difference between written and spoken English disturbs him. 'It was found straight that this was a gross pack between Saturninus and Marius by such as could see day at a little hole.' But precisely that absence of distinction between written and spoken English which serves him so well in simple narratives leaves him uncertain in the presence of more subtle matter. Niceties of psychology and intricacies of argument are blunted by his prose. We have only to imagine him engaged in rendering Thucydides to see his limitation. His task was to make English of one of the greatest story-books in the world; and he did it better than any one else has done.

VII

SHAKESPEARE'S DEDICATION

At some time in the middle fifteen-eighties Shakespeare came to London in search of a livelihood, and more: in search of the means to re-establish the fortunes of his family. We may guess that he arrived in London by 1586, we may make more or less plausible conjectures concerning the manner of his occupation after his arrival; but the one thing we *know* is that in 1593 he had written a beautiful, and within its limits, a masterly poem, *Venus and Adonis*, and that he was dedicating it to a young nobleman, the Earl of Southampton, in language which, though it may sound unduly humble to us who regard Shakespeare as one of the wonders of the world, would sound with dignity and independence surprising to an Elizabethan ear.

Compare the language in which Shakespeare addressed the young Earl of Southampton with that of a dedication made at the same time to the same young nobleman by a writer who lacked neither courage nor genius—Thomas Nashe. Nashe's language is fulsome; to-day it is comic in its exaggeration, but then it was natural. 'Incomprehensible', says Nashe to Southampton, 'is the height of your spirit, both in heroical resolution and matters of conceit. Unreprievably perisheth that book whatsoever to waste paper, which on the diamond rock of your judgment disasterly chanceth to be shipwrackt. . . .' But thus Shakespeare:

'Right Honourable, I know not how I shall offend in dedicating my unpolisht lines to your Lordship, nor how the worlde will censure mee for choosing so strong a proppe to support so weake a burthen, onelye if your Honour seem but pleased, I account my selfe highly praised, and vowe to take advantage of all idle houres, till I have honoured you with some graver labour. But if the first heire of my invention prove deformed, I shall be sorie it had so noble a god-father: and never after eare so barren a land, for feare it yeeld me still so bad a harvest. I leave it to your Honourable survey, and your Honor to your heart's content which I wish may alwaies answere your owne wish, and the world's hopefull expectation.

'Your Honor's in all dutie,
'William Shakespeare.'

Surely, this dedication is, in its kind, a lovely thing. We may say that Shakespeare had the knack of making all things lovely, and that it is merely a trick of the golden pen by which the marriage of deference and dignity is accomplished. I have no great belief in the effect of a trick of the pen; I think that even in so seeming slight a matter as the grace of this dedication, more than a trick was required: some motion of the heart as well. And we may note that Shakespeare, in promising some graver labour if *Venus and Adonis* be well received, is careful to promise only what he can perform. He will take advantage of all *idle* hours. He is a journeyman of the theatre who can give no more than his spare time to the composition of poems for his patron. That he will give; and that, so far as we can tell, he did give. In another year, the graver labour was accomplished: *The Rape of Lucrece*. The dedication is brief, and the tone is changed.

'The love I dedicate to your Lordship is without end: whereof this Pamphlet without beginning is but a superfluous Moity. The warrant I have of your Honourable disposition, not the worth of my untutord Lines makes it assured of acceptance. What I have done is yours, what I have to doe is yours, being part in all I have, devoted yours. Were my worth greater, my duety would show greater, meane time, as it is, it is bound to your Lordship; To whom I wish long life still lengthned with all happinesse.

'Your Lordship's in all duety.

'William Shakespeare.'

This time it is not lines that are dedicated, but love; and the careful devotion of 'all idle hours' gives way to the large surrender: 'What I have done is yours, what I have to do is yours, being part in all I have, devoted yours.' A dedication is, indeed, far removed from a confession. Yet it is hard, and for me impossible, to believe that the words of the second dedication coming from the writer of the first have not their intimate meaning. There was a progress in dedication.

It happens that this word 'dedicate' was one of Shakespeare's favourite words. He obtained from it, in his poetry, some of his most beautiful effects. Of these one or two, at least, will come unaided to the memory of the reader: the others will be glanced at in this essay one by one. For the history of this lovely word in Shakespeare seems to me of some significance.

Before the dedication of *Venus and Adonis* to the Earl of Southampton in 1593, the words 'dedicate' and 'dedication' are nowhere to be found in his plays. Probably, none of these plays was altogether his play, and he meant what he said when he called *Venus and Adonis* 'the first heir of his invention'. It was the child of his invention, whereas the earlier plays had been invented before he put his hand to them. But in them his handiwork is plentiful; yet the word 'dedicate', which he was to use so exquisitely, is not in it. For young Clifford's speech at the end of the second part of *Henry VI* (v. ii. 31), which contains the word, is manifestly an addition made to the play in or about

1598. There is nearly ten years' difference between the rhythm and diction of lines 31–53 and those of the surrounding verses.

The word 'dedicate' enters Shakespeare's vocabulary in 1593, and the occasion is his actual dedication of his first book; it next appears a year later, in 1594, when he dedicates his second book to the same man. Southampton had been pleased with *Venus and Adonis*, and Shakespeare had fulfilled his promise to take advantage of all idle hours. But now he dedicated not merely his new poem, not merely his love, but all himself—'all I am, devoted yours'.

Was he serious? It is impossible for me to read the Sonnets as courtly exercises in compliment. I am one of those who must believe that 'with this key Shakespeare unlocked his heart'. The change of tone between the two actual dedications of *Venus* and *Lucrece* only confirms me in the supposition I find necessary. And the beautiful sonnet—the only one—in which the word occurs (No. 82) gives still more colour to this belief that Shakespeare took his act of dedication seriously.

> I grant thou wert not married to my Muse,
> And therefore may'st without attaint o'erlook
> The dedicated words that poets use
> Of their fair subject, blessing every book.
> Thou art as fair in knowledge as in hue,
> Finding thy worth a limit past my praise,
> And therefore art enforced to seek anew
> Some fresher stamp of the time-bettering days.
> And do so, love; yet when they have devised
> What strained touches rhetoric can lend,
> Thou truly fair wert truly sympathiz'd
> In true plain words by thy true-telling friend;
>   And their gross painting might be better used
>   Where cheeks need blood; in thee it is abused.

Shakespeare is speaking here not of sonnets, but of dedications; and the signs are that he is hurt. In his dedications he has spoken the truth, and truth in Southampton's case is all the grace that is needed. He is disappointed that his young patron is beguiled by 'the strained touches rhetoric can lend'. Of these we have seen a good example in Nashe's hyperbole of flattery.

'I grant thou wert not married to my Muse', says Shakespeare; but the undertone of implication is that Shakespeare had indulged himself with the belief that he was. And that fits exactly with the situation which the two successive dedications themselves suggest. Shakespeare the man of twenty-nine had fallen in love with the young nobleman of nineteen. A ridiculous thing to do, perhaps. That is a matter of opinion. More important for our present purposes, and for a realization of Shakespeare's nature, is to recognize the fact that such things have happened, do happen, and, so far as we can tell, always will happen.

The evidence, as I read it, is that Shakespeare's dedications had been very serious indeed. When he said to the young Earl that all that he was, was devoted his, he meant it. We may say that he was cheating himself, and that he was investing the relation of patron and poet with the glamour of illusion. The real point, if that be our judgement, is that Shakespeare was the kind of man who needed to invest with the glamour of real devotion the equivocal, and often merely sordid, relation between patron and poet. He believed not merely what he wanted, but what he needed, to believe. He loved his young patron, and the act of dedicating his poems to him was an act, not of the calculating mind, but of the heart and soul.

The simple facts are in harmony with this supposition. Never again to the end of his life did Shakespeare dedicate a volume to any man. What he had done, for Southampton, he had done once for all. Whatever happened between them, this act of his should stand alone. Again, we may say, pure accident; it simply happened that Shakespeare wrote no more poems, and wrote no more dedications. It is possible. I am merely concerned to point out that the terms of the dedications themselves, the tone of the sonnet which speaks of the dedications, and the fact that Shakespeare dedicated no more, fall into natural and unforced harmony with the story whose outlines we gather from the sequence of the Sonnets themselves.

Not only are these simple facts thus in natural harmony, but the more delicate evidences to which we have already alluded. Before the actual dedication of *Venus and Adonis*, the word 'dedicate' is nowhere to be found in Shakespeare's plays. In the actual dedications and in the sonnet which speaks of them, the word is used simply: Shakespeare dedicates his book; then he dedicates his love; then all that he is. There is progressive dedication. The new word takes on a depth of intimate meaning.

With a suddenness almost startling 'dedicate' becomes a precious word in Shakespeare's language. A little while before it did not exist, now it is elected to convey the tenderest and most exquisite meanings. We have only to listen. It describes the birth of love in Romeo.

> But he, his own affection's counsellor,
> Is to himself—I will not say how true—
> But to himself so secret and so close,
> So far from sounding or discovery,
> As is the bud bit by the envious worm,
> Ere he can spread his sweet leaves in the air
> Or *dedicate* his beauty to the sun. (I. i. 158.)

Or, in *Twelfth Night*, it springs from Shakespeare's mind to describe the disappointed Antonio's devotion to Sebastian.

> A witchcraft drew me hither:
> That most ungrateful boy there by your side,
> From the rude sea's enraged and foamy mouth
> Did I redeem; a wreck past hope he was:
> His life I gave him and did thereto add
> My love, without retention or restraint,
> *All in his dedication.* (v. i. 86.)

We cannot escape the echo: 'What I have done is yours; what I have to do is yours; being part in all I have, devoted yours.' Or, in a lighter vein, it is used by Benedick in *Much Ado* to describe Claudio's infatuation for Hero, while he is blind to his own for Beatrice.

> 'I do much wonder that one man seeing how much another man is a fool when he *dedicates his behaviours to love* will, after he hath laughed at such follies in others, become the argument of his own scorn by falling in love.' (II. iii. 9.)

'Dedication' and love appear to be part of a single thought, or a single experience. A natural collocation, it may be said. Natural or not, it was unknown to Shakespeare's language before he dedicated to Southampton. And who can tell whether it is not largely by the magic of Shakespeare's language that the collocation seems so natural to us to-day?

Or again the image from the description of Romeo in love as the bud bit by the envious worm ere he 'can dedicate his beauty to the sun' appears, magically changed, in the picture of Henry V on the morning before Agincourt.

For forth he goes and visits all his host,
Bids them good-morrow with a modest smile,
And calls them brothers, friends, and countrymen.
Upon his royal face there is no note
How dread an army hath enrounded him;
Now doth he *dedicate one jot of colour*
Unto the weary and all-watched night. (IV, chor. 37.)

There beauty and valour are one. In young Clifford's thrilling speech at the end of *2 Henry VI* it is to valour alone that dedication is made; but what dedication is, is plainly and passionately declared.

O war, thou son of Hell,
Whom angry heavens do make their minister,
Throw in the frozen bosoms of our part
Hot coals of vengeance! Let no soldier fly.
He that is *truly dedicate to war*
Hath no self-love, nor he that loves himself
Hath not essentially, but by circumstance,
The name of valour. (V. ii. 37.)

Dedication is utter self-surrender, to love, to valour, or, in Isabella's lovely words to Angelo in *Measure for Measure*, to God.

Isab. Hark how I'll bribe you: good my lord, turn back.
Ang. How! bribe me?
Isab. Ay, with such gifts that heaven shall share with you.
Not with fond shekels of the tested gold,
Or stones whose rates are either rich or poor
As fancy values them; but with true prayers
That shall be up at heaven and enter there
Ere sun-rise, prayers from preserved souls,
From fasting maids *whose minds are dedicate*
To nothing temporal. (II. ii. 154.)

Already we have chronicled every occasion on which the word 'dedicate' is used by Shakespeare from the time of his dedication of *Venus and Adonis* until *Measure for Measure*. We have omitted none. Can it be mere accident that we have compiled a tiny anthology of perfect felicities? Or does not the experience rather confirm our surmise that the word itself was precious?

Can it be mere accident again that the word which has been used to express such exquisite or heroic self-devotions suddenly takes on a sinister meaning? It is now Cressida's word, at the moment when Troilus is aching to believe that his integrity and truth to her (his 'dedication', in fact)

> Might be affronted by the match and weight
> Of such a winnow'd purity in love.
>
> (III. ii. 174.)

It is Troilus, alas, who is dedicated; but it is Cressida who speaks the word.

> *Pan.* What, blushing still? Have you not done talking yet?
> *Cres.* Well, uncle, what folly I commit, I *dedicate* to you.
>
> (III. ii. 109.)

Or it describes the fearful disillusion of Timon, bitten by the rankling tooth of man's ingratitude.

> 1 *Serv.* So noble a master fall'n. All gone! and not
> One friend to take his fortune by the arm,
> And go along with him.
> 2 *Serv.* As we do turn our backs
> From our companion thrown into his grave,
> So his familiars to his buried fortunes
> Slink all away, leave their false vows with him,
> Like empty purses picked; and his poor self,
> *A dedicated beggar to the air*,
> With his disease of all-shunned poverty,
> Walks, like contempt, alone. (IV. ii. 13.)

The poetry is superb; the use of the word magnificent. But the human emotion how changed! We cannot but remember the former dedication to the air, of which the rose-bud in *Romeo* was cheated. We remember too the false vows of Cressida. It may be mere accident that somewhere in the background of 'dedication' seems to hover a suggestion of treachery. And the same suggestion creeps out again in the use of the word in *Cymbeline*, where it forms part of Iachimo's loathsome suggestion to Imogen, and his treachery to Posthumus.

Imo. Revenged!
How should I be revenged? If this be true—
As I have such a heart that both mine ears
Must not in haste abuse—if it be true,
How should I be revenged?
Iach. Should he make me
Live, like Diana's priest, between cold sheets,
Whiles he is vaulting variable ramps,
In your respite, upon your purse? Revenge it.
I dedicate myself to your sweet pleasure. (I. vi. 136.)

The word, it seems, could suffer no greater defilement than this. Yet perhaps in *Macbeth* it does, in the scene where Malcolm makes trial of Macduff. Macduff is being bitterly disillusioned while Malcolm tells of his vices. 'There 's no bottom, none, in my voluptuousness', says Malcolm. With weary cynicism Macduff replies:

Boundless intemperance
In nature is a tyranny; it hath been
The untimely emptying of the happy throne,
And fall of many kings. But fear not yet
To take upon you what is yours: you may
Convey your pleasures in a spacious plenty,
And yet seem cold, the time you may so hoodwink.
We have willing dames enough; there cannot be
That vulture in you, to devour so many
As will to greatness dedicate themselves,
Finding it so inclined. (IV. iii. 75.)

The use here touches an absolute of revulsion. The word is trampled on in the cold and ghastly joke of such 'a dedication to greatness'. The transvaluation of values is complete.

After that, the mere suggestion of yielding oneself up to a desperate and forlorn adventure is even comfortable. Thus the word is used, in a passage of pure poetic beauty, in the *Winter's Tale*, when Camillo warns Florizel against

> *A wild dedication of yourselves*
> *To unpath'd waters*, undream'd shores, most certain
> To miseries enough: no hope to help you,
> But as you shake off one to take another;
> Nothing so certain as your anchors, who
> Do their best office if they can but stay you
> Where you'll be loath to be. (IV. iv. 579.)

The final use of the word, in *The Tempest*, is in Prospero's story to Miranda.

> I, thus neglecting worldly ends, *all dedicated*
> *To closeness and the bettering of my mind*
> With that, which, but by being so retired,
> O'erprized all popular rate, in my false brother
> Awaked an evil nature. (I. ii. 89.)

Dedication and treachery seem still to be close companions. But now the dedication itself is pure again; the word itself is no longer contaminated, as it was by Cressida and Iachimo and in *Macbeth*. It is simply that the dedicated soul is simple and by the fact of its dedication laid open to treachery. That is 'the mystery of iniquity', and not even in *The Tempest* could Shakespeare solve it. He recognized it simply as a condition of an order of existence from which men must free themselves.

We have followed precisely the history of the word 'dedication' in Shakespeare; we have examined every occasion of its use, save one. Is it mere fancy that impels us to believe that its story is not fortuitous? Till 1593 the word is unknown in Shakespeare; it appears then, quite simply, in two actual dedications, to the same young nobleman to whom the sonnets were written. These were the only dedications—or shall we say the only dedication?—which Shakespeare ever made. Hard upon this the word enters on a period of delicate metaphorical life, during which it is inseparably connected with true and complete devotion. 'Dedication' holds the beauty of devotion: it is a beauty of language to describe a beauty of soul.

Abruptly there is a change in its human quality. It is given over to cynicism, and made the accomplice of treachery. Dedication is no longer to love, but to lust; no longer of love, but of lust. Or the dedicated man, like Timon, is betrayed by his friends, or, like Prospero, by his brother; or the outcast and desperate man is dedicated to the air, or to the wild waters. Can it be all pure accident that the lovely suggestion of the word is now altogether lost? Is it simply that in plays of 'the tragic period' even a word must suffer a little tragedy of its own? The answer will not suffice. Iachimo need not have 'dedicated' himself to Imogen, nor Macduff have caricatured the high associations of the word. The degradation here, at least, was deliberate, even though it were unconscious. Shakespeare is turning the barb in the wound.

What was the wound? How was it caused, and by whom was it caused? Perhaps the answer may be sought in the one remaining use of the word which we have so far forborne to chronicle. It is in *Timon*, and it comes at the very opening of that strange play. The poet, with the painter, and the jeweller, and the merchant, is standing in the great man's ante-room. Suddenly, the poet begins reciting to himself some lines which the painter indistinctly overhears.

Pain. You are rapt, sir, in some work, some dedication
To the great lord.
Poet. A thing slipp'd idly from me.
Our poesy is as a gum which oozes
From whence 'tis nourish'd: the fire i' the flint
Shows not till it be struck; our gentle flame
Provokes itself, and like the current flies
Each bound it chafes. What have you there?
Pain. A picture, sir. When comes your book forth?
Poet. Upon the heels of my presentment, sir. (I. i. 19.)

The situation is clear. The poet has dedicated his book, and it waits only for formal presentation to the great lord to be made public. The presentation is accomplished two lines later in the scene.

Poet. Vouchsafe my labour, and long live your lordship!
Tim. I thank you; you shall hear from me anon:
Go not away. (I. i. 153.)

So the poet awaits his reward from Timon's treasurer. While he is waiting, he accosts Apemantus.

Poet. How now, philosopher!
Apem. Thou liest.
Poet. Art not one?
Apem. Yes.
Poet. Then I lie not.
Apem. Art not a poet?
Poet. Yes.
Apem. Then thou liest: look in thy last work, where thou hast feigned him a worthy fellow.
Poet. That 's not feigned; he is so. (I. i. 221.)

The poet is obviously sincere. His long previous talk with the painter shows him convinced of Timon's 'good and gracious nature'. It is not Timon who is unworthy, but 'the glib and slippery creatures' whom his wealth attracts to seeming service. Not merely the poet's own expressed opinion, but the whole theme and conduct of the play make it impossible that Timon should have been in his mind, when the thing slipped idly from him. The thing itself is memorable, because it sticks out clear from the course and sense of the scene.

Poet. [*Reciting to himself.*] 'When we for recompense have praised the vile,
It stains the glory in that happy verse
Which aptly sings the good.' (I. i. 15.)

Either it is totally irrelevant, or the connexion is that the thought of his dedication to the good Timon, whom he has aptly sung in happy verse, reminds the poet of a former dedication, wherein he praised the vile for recompense. By this past soil his sincere praise is now stained.

So, at the turning-point of the history of the word 'dedication' in Shakespeare's poetry, we find that it abruptly descends from the heaven of metaphor to the earth of sordid experience. Only here, at the beginning of *Timon*, since it first entered Shakespeare's vocabulary, does the word return to its direct and most familiar use on the lips of a writer: the dedication of a book. There is nothing divine, nothing beautiful, nothing ideal about it. At this moment 'dedication' is prostitution: 'when we for recompense have praised the vile', and a prostitution that leaves behind it an enduring stain. And as we have seen, if there is one predominant strain in the later meaning of 'dedication' in Shakespeare's poetry, it is precisely this of prostitution. On the lips of Cressida, of Macduff, and Iachimo this is, in the earthliest sense, its meaning.

Cymbeline is among the very latest plays of Shakespeare. *Timon*, *Troilus*, and *Macbeth* we cannot date precisely. They belong roughly together, and the accepted date for them is anything between 1606 and 1609. Did anything happen between those dates which might have made the word 'dedication' suddenly turn to ashes in Shakespeare's mouth?

Something did happen then, and so far as we can tell at this distance of time, it was the one thing which must have had precisely this effect. In 1609 Shakespeare's intimate sonnets were published to the world. To Shakespeare, whose plays reveal him as beyond all men of his time (or of ours) sensitive in this matter of love, the publication must have been a fearful violation. And, ultimately, Southampton must have been responsible for it. Whether it was in deliberate malice, or indifferent contempt, or mere carelessness, that he allowed those sonnets to fall into the hands of an unscrupulous publisher, would have made no difference to the effect on Shakespeare of this publication. Malice in such an issue would be no worse than carelessness, although in fact carelessness is hardly conceivable.

What Shakespeare's relations with Southampton had been for the dozen years before the catastrophe of publication, we can only guess. The passionate infatuation had certainly cooled, and probably there was real estrangement. The young nobleman, as he passed from youth to manhood, learned that his attachment to a poet and a strolling player was a thing to be forgotten. Shakespeare would have acquiesced in the necessity, and consoled himself with the thought that in each remained a memory of what had been. But when, perhaps many months before their actual publication, he learned that his sonnets had been handed over to the gutter-press of those days, then the last veil of possible illusion was torn away. All that had been was cankered.

The sudden revulsion from the past was fearful; there came a moment of brutal injustice to himself, when it seemed to him not merely that Southampton was vile: but he himself was viler still. He had deliberately deceived his own soul; he had pretended love where he had sought reward; he had not dedicated, but prostituted himself. The self-revelation, though false, was appalling.

[MARCH 1929.

VIII

PROBLEMS OF THE SHAKESPEARE SONNETS

MR. J. M. ROBERTSON has spent many years of a full and distinguished life as *advocatus diaboli* to the canonical Shakespeare. Unfortunately for him, and for ourselves, an intimate knowledge of Shakespeare is comparatively rare among us, so that the value of this patiently thankless labour has not been properly appreciated. Even the most sympathetic critic, reviewing the volumes of Mr. Robertson's work as they have from time to time appeared, is compelled by the nature of the case 'to spend all his might' not in praise of Mr. Robertson's patient scholarship, but in the detailed defence of the Shakesperian canon from his disintegrating skill. And this stubborn and instinctive opposition, in the case of the sympathetic and appreciative critic, is not mere obscurantism. The Shakespearian canon must be defended as long as a real defence is possible. The *a priori* case for it is so strong that the Shakespearian critic needs to be convinced that the case against it is really stronger, before he can fairly yield a position. Heminge and Condell, who put together the Folio, were genuine intimates of Shakespeare; and we are compelled to conclude that they would have admitted nothing into the Folio which did not pass among the King's men for 'Shakespeare's play'.

But we are equally compelled to conclude that what the phrase 'Shakespeare's play' meant to a leader of the King's men was not at all the same thing as the phrase would convey to a modern man. It can have meant no more to them than that the play was more

Shakespeare's than anybody else's; and 'more his' can only have meant that his claim to the final fashioning was preponderant. Whether that final fashioning was a mere touching-up or a complete rewriting of other men's work, or a new and independent creation, is for the critic to decide. Whether, having decided, he can persuade other critics of the rightness of his decision, is another matter. What needs to be emphasized is that the critical 'disintegration' of Shakespeare is a legitimate occupation: it is not, as it is so often represented, a manifestation of critical perversity. Moreover, besides being legitimate, it is positively helpful. It compels the conservative opponent to bring into the clear light of consciousness his own uncriticized assumptions.

This process of self-examination which Mr. Robertson enforces upon the Shakespearian critic is, it seems to us, altogether salutary; and we may conceive him as a kind of Cato the Censor in the rather lax republic of Shakespeare criticism. Whether such a Cato is exactly the best person to decide whether or not at a given moment Shakespeare is being true to himself may be doubted; but since no one but a Cato would undertake the ill-rewarded task, and Catos are scarce, we ought to congratulate ourselves on possessing a Shakespearian critic so resolute and so disinterested as Mr. Robertson. Only when we have made quite clear our deep sense of gratitude to Mr. Robertson do we feel morally free to submit his work to that critical examination which it is its main purpose to provoke. His latest book on Shakespeare's Sonnets,[1] affords an admirable opportunity for the work. His previous volumes on the Shakespearian canon

---

[1] THE PROBLEMS OF THE SHAKESPEARE SONNETS. By the *Rt. Hon. J. M. Robertson.* (Routledge.)

agitate too many and too diverse problems for brief examination. They are books which call for books in reply. The question of the Sonnets is compact and self-enclosed.

Mr. Robertson's ostensible point of departure in his criticism of the Sonnets is the inclusion in the Thorpe Quarto of *The Lover's Complaint* with a definite ascription of it to Shakespeare. Mr. Mackail has denied that *The Lover's Complaint* is Shakespeare's work; Mr. Robertson agrees and goes farther: he says it is the work of Chapman. (This verdict we consider eminently reasonable, in the sense that, if *The Lover's Complaint* had been found as an anonymous Elizabethan poem, it would have been ascribed to Chapman long ago.) From this Mr. Robertson argues that the authority of the Thorpe Quarto, once shaken in respect of *The Lover's Complaint*, is suspect in respect of the Sonnets. In other words, the Thorpe Quarto is in the same position as the Folio; and Mr. Robertson's treatment of it is accordingly a miniature version of his treatment of the Folio. And, of course, the resistance to his criticism will be of the same kind in this case as in that: a resistance based on the fear, familiar in Biblical criticism, that once a breach of any kind is made in the traditional canon no end can be set to the process of disintegration.

And Mr. Robertson certainly carries the process far. Thus he begins by confidently denying that Sonnet XX—'A woman's face with Nature's own hand painted'—is Shakespeare's; goes on to claim that Sonnets LXIX and LXX are by Chapman; and, in the final count,

'sees reason to doubt, more or less strongly, the Shakespearian authorship of more than forty Sonnets in what may be termed Part I of the Quarto [i.e. 1–126]; and to interpret as very probably addressed to a woman, or women, some thirty-two, instead of following the time-honoured practice of treating all save the merely reflective as addressed to one man.'

From the remainder ten or a dozen are rejected: in all between fifty and sixty are branded. A kind of Black Death sweeps through the Quarto.

Nerving Mr. Robertson's arm to this vigorous, even ruthless, application of the knife is a passionate idealization of Shakespeare. Shakespeare, Mr. Robertson is convinced, cannot have been guilty of inferior work; and the sonnets which he rejects he holds to be inferior. But inferior is a vague conception. Many would admit that there are a number of inferior sonnets in the first section of the Quarto; but many who admit this would insist that such inferiority is seldom absolute but almost always relative, and they would reject the deduction that such inferiority is evidence that these sonnets are not Shakespeare's work. They will abide by their old argument that there is plenty of inferior work in *Venus and Adonis* and *The Rape of Lucrece*, an argument which is not seriously disturbed by Mr. Robertson's contention that the two narrative poems were deliberate 'best-sellers', whereas the Sonnets were written by Shakespeare for the satisfaction of his soul. For here once again the question has been begged. The natural impression produced by some of the Sonnets certainly is that they were deliberate and rather exaggerated panegyrics upon a young and aristocratic recipient. Perhaps it is this notion which offends Mr. Robertson. We may sympathize with this sensitiveness for Shakespeare's reputation; but we can do no more. We cannot accept it as a touchstone of what is authentic Shakespeare. For the evidence is that Shakespeare was infatuated, and his young patron exacting. He was 'fond in praise, which made his praises worse'. It is surely faintly preposterous to expect that Shakespeare should have refused, on moral or aesthetic grounds, to indulge him. After all, their intimacy—between a young member of the high nobility and an obscure poet-player—was in those days an extraordinary thing; and to Shakespeare, even in its most glamorous moments, it must have appeared like a glancing bubble which only by some precarious miracle was not broken. To our reverential eyes it was Shakespeare who was the great lord, and Southampton the privileged intimate; but our vision is distorted. Socially the young Earl was infinitely exalted above Shakespeare. That is easy to see. What is harder to remember is that, psychologically, in such a relation even between social equals it is the older man who is the slave. In such circumstances, we should expect that a fair proportion of the Sonnets would be poetically inferior. Some of them were bound to be hack-work, not a whit less arduous because the command came from an imperious young aristocrat and not the general public. It is only when this inferiority reaches an extreme point that we have any reasonable justification for denying a sonnet to Shakespeare.

Let us take as a specimen of Mr. Robertson's method his treatment of Sonnet xx.

A woman's face with Nature's own hand painted
Hast thou, the master-mistress of my passion;
A woman's gentle heart, but not acquainted
With shifting change, as is false women's fashion;
An eye more bright than theirs, less false in rolling,
Gilding the object whereupon it gazeth;
A man in hue, all hues in his controlling,
Which steals men's eyes and women's souls amazeth.

And for a woman wert thou first created;
Till Nature, as she wrought thee, fell a-doting,
And by addition me of thee defeated,
By adding one thing to my purpose nothing.
  But since she pricked thee out for women's pleasure,
  Mine be thy love and thy love's use their treasure.

Mr. Robertson does not like the sonnet; he would like to be rid of it, as many others would. For our own part, we confess we see nothing heinous in it; after all, it is a light-hearted affair, and, if swallowed without anticipatory grimaces, leaves nothing very unpleasant in the after-taste. It is, it need hardly be said, not a distinguished sonnet; it belongs to the class of *jeux d'esprit.* But to have persuaded oneself that it is not the sort of joke that the Shakespeare of *Love's Labour's Lost* would have made seems uncritical, for the obvious bawdy pun in the final couplet is a pun of which Berowne and Mercutio at least were demonstrably fond. On the whole, we should say that the *a priori* case for its being Shakespeare's sonnet was strong enough. Mr. Robertson, however, misliking it, wants to get rid of it. He does this by means of the line—

Which steals men's eyes and women's souls *amazeth.*

The word 'amazeth', he says, directly recalls Barnabe Barnes; and he quotes from Barnes's *Parthenophil*:

In looking on thy face, whose sight amazes
My sense.

together with three other uses of 'amaze' from Barnes's sonnet-sequence. But such an argument could only have force if Shakespeare did not elsewhere use the word 'amaze'. On the contrary, he uses it repeatedly, and the use of it in one line in *Venus and Adonis*

sweet lips and crystal eyne,
whose full perfection all the world amazes—

is much nearer to the use in Sonnet xx than anything Mr. Robertson quotes from Barnes. Yet, having quoted the line from *Venus and Adonis*, Mr. Robertson proceeds: 'that Shakespeare has so echoed Barnes's four-times repeated tag is really a ground for inferring it was not he who used it a sixth time in a Barnesian sonnet.' That argument is simply bewildering; for there is, on the face of it, no reason at all for supposing that Shakespeare is echoing Barnes, or echoing anybody. 'Amaze' is not an utterly original word. Further, the only reason we can see for calling it a 'Barnesian sonnet' is this use of 'amazes', which is no reason at all. It is a far more mellifluous sonnet than any by the hapless Barnes.

Here, it seems clear, the wish has been father to the thought with Mr. Robertson: an anxious desire to dissociate Shakespeare from what many consider an equivocal sonnet has disguised itself (rather transparently) as a stylistic judgement. And the same moral scruple is elsewhere at work, consciously or unconsciously, in Mr. Robertson's mind. He is cruelly unfair to Samuel Butler's book on the Sonnets, simply because he is shocked by Butler's theory, though indeed there is nothing particularly shocking in it. There are many extravagances in Butler's book, but his insistence upon the reality of Shakespeare's infatuation for the young man is not one of them.

Mr. Robertson, like many others, does not like to contemplate a Shakespeare infatuated by a young man; like many others he can contemplate with a comparative (but only comparative) equanimity a Shakespeare infatuated by a woman. But the data are stubborn: Shakespeare, on any natural reading of the Sonnets, experienced both infatuations. That is, to put it mildly, a very unusual experience. But, after all, there is, in the astonishing and mysterious body of work which belongs to Shakespeare every ground for supposing that he was capable of unusual experience; and in fact, if we had no Sonnets at all, we should be compelled to deduce some such abnormal 'experiencing nature' in the author of Shakespeare's plays as is exposed to view in the Sonnets. The difficulty most of us feel in imaginatively realizing this nature of Shakespeare's is great; most of us are capable of but one kind of devotion, and capable even of that to a far less devouring extreme than Shakespeare evidently was. We cannot help approaching Shakespeare the man as revealed in the Sonnets from the one side or the other; and, unless we ourselves are capable of an unusual flexibility and openness of mind, we forget that we are fitting Shakespeare to our pattern and not to his. And this, it seems to us, is the fundamental weakness of the conception of Shakespeare upon which Mr. Robertson's critical method ultimately depends. Every serious critic of Shakespeare must have a conception of Shakespeare; every serious critic of Shakespeare should do as honestly and openly as Mr. Robertson what Mr. Robertson does—try his conception against the facts. But when he reaches a result like Mr. Robertson's—namely, a denial that between fifty and sixty of the Sonnets are Shakespeare's at all—it is time for him to ask himself seriously whether his conception is founded on the facts, or the facts are being adjusted to fit the conception.

This, we believe, is what has happened with Mr. Robertson. We find him continually forcing the note in matters of pure literary criticism. Take, for a single example, his treatment of Sonnet LXIX, which we print with the usual emendations of 'end' into 'due' in the third and 'their' into 'thy' in the fifth line:

Those parts of thee that the world's eye doth view
Want nothing that the thought of hearts can mend:
All tongues (the voice of souls) give thee that due
Uttering bare truth, even so as foes commend.
Thy outward thus with outward praise is crowned,
But those same tongues, that give thee so thine own,
In other accents do that praise confound
By seeing farther than the eye hath shown.
They look into the beauty of thy mind,
And that in guess they measure by thy deeds,
Then churls their thoughts (although their eyes were kind)
To thy fair flower add the rank smell of weeds.
  But why thy odour matcheth not thy show,
  The soil is this, that thou dost common grow.

On this Mr. Robertson comments, first, that 'it begins in a flagrantly un-Shakespearian fashion'. Surely there is nothing in the least un-Shakespearian in the rhythm at least of the first four lines. The antithesis between 'the thought of hearts' and 'the voice of souls', being mainly verbal, does not commend itself to modern taste; but that hardly gives us warrant for calling it un-Shakespearian. Mr. Robertson then says that 'the argument of lines 9–12 is so confused that it defies interpretation'. But the interpretation seems simple enough when once it is grasped that 'look into' is used in the sense 'make inquiry into', precisely as it is used in the last lines of the next sonnet but one (No. LXXI).

But let your love even with my life decay,
Lest the wise world should *look into* your moan,
And mock you with me after I am gone.

Neither the conceit by which 'accents' are made 'to see,' nor the slight quibble in the use of 'look into', can fairly be described as un-Shakespearian. And the final comparison between the odour of a flower and the inward truth and beauty of the soul recurs more than once in the Sonnets. Mr. Robertson's conclusion that the Sonnet is a 'compound of crooked reasoning, cramped diction, and unmusical versification, as like Chapman as it is unlike Shakespeare', seems to us far from the truth. One can, of course, only pit opinion against opinion; but the sonnet seems to us as musical as the average Shakespearian sonnet, and quite definitely more musical than any of Chapman's sonnets in *The Coronet.*

We are not contending that the sonnet is a fine sonnet—that it certainly is not—but only that it is such a piece as we might reasonably expect Shakespeare to have written in an indifferent moment, that it is quite definitely unlike Chapman's contorted sonneteering, that the negative arguments would need to be far stronger to prevail against the presumption of authenticity that it enjoys. We need not, and Mr. Robertson shows cogent reason why we need not, suppose that the Quarto is infallible; but to admit the possiblity of a few mistaken ascriptions is by far removed from admitting the probability of wholesale blundering. We are not, as Mr. Robertson seems continually to assume, free to deny to Shakespeare any sonnet in the Quarto which may strike us as inferior to our chosen best. Our assumption, on the contrary, must be that they are Shakespeare's; and we must hold to it until it is demonstrated in each particular case that a sonnet cannot reasonably be attributed to him. From this necessary assumption, it seems to us, Mr. Robertson is continually endeavouring to escape; he wishes to forget it, in order that he may be free to create a Shakespeare after his heart's desire. He wishes to induce in himself and in us the feeling that it is not necessary to presume the authenticity of the sonnets in the Quarto. Sometimes he comes near, by his forthrightness and detailed persistence, to succeeding: then all we can do is to escape from the labyrinth of the trees and take a good look at the wood. Mr. Robertson's Shakespeare is a fine and noble thing, but it is only a part of Shakespeare.

With some of Mr. Robertson's other arguments we are in hearty agreement. We agree with him that the great majority of the Sonnets call imperatively for an early dating on grounds of thought and diction. Of no single one of the Sonnets—not even the famous CVII—would we care to say positively that it was written as late as *Hamlet*. Not even the finest of the Sonnets display that inimitable flexibility of phrase which we associate with Shakespeare's full maturity. It may be argued that the Shakespearian sonnet gives no opportunity for this; but we believe that Shakespeare, had he been writing sonnets at the time of *Hamlet*, would easily have made the form yield the opportunity. Of such convictions it is never easy to convince others; but this particular view that the Sonnets must be dated early is borne out by the only piece of definite evidence we possess—namely, the printing of Sonnets CXXXVIII and CXLIV in *The Passionate Pilgrim* of 1598. These two Sonnets at least must have been written before that date; and these same two Sonnets, judged by their content, belong to the latest sonnet stratum. What is of the utmost importance, they show Shakespeare describing himself as 'old', his 'days past the best', at an age when he was demonstrably not more than thirty-three. There are no sonnets in the Quarto (with the possible but no means certain exception of CVII[1]) which can, on

[1] See note, p. 201.

convincing internal evidence, be placed considerably later than these two; and we are free to suppose that these, and the rest of the Sonnets with them, were written well before 1598.

Mr. Robertson's further contention, wherein he follows Professor Minto, and (with the discretion necessary) Mr. Arthur Acheson, that the rival poet was Chapman is again one which we accept. It surely is hardly possible for any one to read through Chapman's early poems with an open and careful mind without coming to the definite conclusions first, that he is the poet hit off with such brilliant and debonair good humour in the lines

> He nor that affable familiar ghost
> That nightly gulls him with intelligence—

and, second, that Chapman is, in his poems, incessantly girding at a successful rival poet who has established himself in the favour of a nobleman by poems which Chapman condemns as sensual. Much of the evidence already propounded with pardonable exaggeration by Mr. Acheson is reasonably and forcefully restated by Mr. Robertson; to it we venture to add the lines of the second part of *The Shadow of Night*, where Chapman, after singing the praises of Cynthia, the Goddess of Night (the half-poem is entitled *Hymnus in Cynthiam*), with something more than his characteristic inconsequence, exclaims:

> Presume not then ye flesh-confounded souls,
> That cannot bear the full Castalian bowls,
> Which sever mounting spirits from their senses,
> To look in this deep fount for thy pretences.

The change of 'ye' to 'thy' betrays that Chapman is hitting at an individual; and, in our opinion, the whole passage will bear no meaning save as an angry reference to the couplet of Ovid:

> Vilia miretur vulgus: mihi flavus Apollo
> Pocula Castalia plena ministret aqua,

which is the superscription of Shakespeare's *Venus and Adonis*.

If the identification of the rival poet with Chapman be accepted, as we believe it eventually must, on purely literary grounds, we have a fairly certain date for some of the most assured and masterly of Shakespeare's Sonnets. The rival poet series then belongs to 1593 or 1594; and with 1598 for a certain *terminus ante quem*, we may fairly conclude that our natural deductions from the stylistic evidence—namely, that the Sonnets date roughly from 1592 to 1597–8—will not be controverted by any external evidence save that which is manufactured to suit the claims of some particular person as 'onlie begetter', or as 'dark lady'. No real investigation of the problems of the Sonnets can be based on these hazardous assumptions; and besides, the actual identity of Shakespeare's 'good' and 'bad angels' is a matter of minor importance. But the importance of the fact that they existed, and that they occupied Shakespeare's mind and soul at a definite and ascertainable period of his life, is considerable.

IX

JACQUES-BÉNIGNE BOSSUET

(1627–1704)

PROBABLY Bossuet is little more to most men of to-day than the author of *Oraisons Funèbres*; and of those funeral orations the best known to Englishmen is the one which is intimately concerned with our history—the panegyric of Henrietta Maria, the Queen of Charles I. It was composed by Bossuet in the first full maturity of his splendid powers; it is often cited as the highest achievement of human eloquence. Its pathos, its majesty, its dramatic force, its contrasts, and its exquisite modulations from the sudden surprise of 'Un homme s'est rencontré . . .' to the gentle and unemphatic close—all these qualities make their impression upon even the schoolboy reader. It is a monument of art, and an art of which we feel, truly enough, that we have long since lost the secret.

Yet this same oration on Queen Henrietta Maria, if it is more closely regarded, yields something more than the excuse for a detached, if not a resentful, aesthetic admiration. If it receives only that from us, it is itself degraded; it becomes a *tour de force*, and the great Bishop something of the mere performer. And those many critics who, like Brunetière, have lauded the 'lyric genius' of Bossuet, can hardly escape this condemnation. To admire Bossuet solely for his 'lyricism'—whatever that may mean—is an impertinence. The one oration is enough to reveal the inadequacy of such an attitude. The quality of which we are chiefly conscious in it is one of design and control: the oration is marshalled. But it is not enough to say that the art is deliberate. Deliberate art is hardly more than a phrase. No art is more deliberate than painting miniatures. Bossuet's deliberate art is concerned with the deaths of kings and the revolution of nations. So, it may be said, is high tragedy, for which Bossuet cared so little. But there was no room for tragedy in his philosophy; there could be none. The question was not for him whether Samson had quit himself like Samson, but whether he was saved or damned. Tragedy for its own sake was meaningless to him, and the idea of it almost as remote from him as that of 'lyricism' for its own sake would have been. These conceptions are of a period to which Bossuet did not belong; and to blame him, as one of his most whole-hearted modern French admirers blames him, for misunderstanding the rationale of tragedy and ignoring the force of Aristotle's defence of it is merely to show that it is very hard for a modern mind, even if sympathetic, to enter into Bossuet's completeness.

A complete philosophy of life must solve the problem of evil. There are only two such philosophies; and they are mutually exclusive. One is the philosophy of Christian orthodoxy, the other the philosophy of tragedy. Bossuet was probably the last great European mind which embraced, without doubt or reservation and therefore without inconsistency, the former. Sainte-Beuve, in a famous phrase, described him sweepingly as 'l'âme la moins combattue qui fût jamais au monde'; and though the justice of the description has been challenged, and will be challenged here, there is singularly little trace, even in his earliest writings, of any moral struggle in Bossuet. He grew naturally, almost gaily to judge by his early sermons, into the great philosophy of orthodoxy. As his powers expanded they found complete satisfaction and activity within the Catholic faith.

His mind was broad and deep, a truly magnificent mind; but he was not a great metaphysician. His sense of the concrete reality was too strong to permit him to plunge for long into the delights of abstract thought. Not the world of ideas, but the world of history, was his home; not the world of epistemology, but the world of moral effort was what he looked to in man. These he sought to comprehend, and these he comprehended. The meaning of the long historical process lay in the foundation and gradual victory of the visible Church; the meaning of the individual life lay in the gradual approach to God by the means visibly ordained for that approach. He proclaims his certainty, with the accent of certainty, in the oration upon Madame:

> 'En effet, jusqu'à ce que nous ayons trouvé la véritable sagesse; tant que nous regardons l'homme par les yeux du corps, sans y démêler par l'intelligence ce secret principe de toutes nos actions, qui, étant capable de s'unir à Dieu, doit nécessairement y retourner, que verrons-nous autre chose ıs notre vie que de folles inquiétudes? . . . Voulez-vous oir en un mot ce que c'est que l'homme? Tout son devoir, ut son objet, toute sa nature, c'est de craindre Dieu: tout ıe reste est vain, je le déclare; mais aussi tout le reste n'est pas l'homme.'

'Il est donc maintenant', Bossuet continues, with a phrase that is deeply characteristic of him, 'aisé de concilier toutes choses.' The mystery of grace in the individual soul explains the universe. Bossuet meant it, and to the uttermost. 'Pour la donner à l'Église', he goes on to declare of Madame, 'il a fallu renverser tout un royaume.' To a modern ear it sounds like rhetorical hyperbole; and so long as it sounds so to us, we have not entered into communion with a great mind. If there is paradox in such a statement, it was for Bossuet the paradox of true mystery; he was justifying the ways of God to man, and they were at once mysterious and plain to him. Just as the misfortunes of her mother and the English Civil War had their origin in the schism of an English king, so in order that Madame be saved to the true Church it was necessary that her father's house be overthrown. It is easy enough to smile at such a philosophy, or such a faith; fatally easy for a Voltaire to fasten upon aspects of it which may be made to appear ridiculous in the crude glare of a mere rationalism, to raise a laugh over the nakedness with which Bossuet sometimes uttered it in his *Histoire Universelle*. 'Jephté ensanglante sa victoire par un sacrifice qui ne peut être excusé que par un ordre secret de Dieu, sur lequel il ne lui a pas plu de nous rien faire connaître.' But let us not deceive ourselves into supposing that Bossuet was unconscious of the difficulty. To impute naivety to Bossuet is to reveal our own. Bossuet in such a sentence shows the candour of his soul. There was something to be explained, and he explained it. We may not like the explanation, but we must admire the honesty of it. More than this: even if we can no longer accept the philosophy of faith, we can at least bring ourselves to understand that it satisfies some sense in man that a mere rationalism can never satisfy, the sense of the wonder and the mystery of the world, the strangeness of the things which are.

Over rationalism Bossuet soars triumphant. He knew the enemy well enough; *libertins* were not rare in his day; but not the greatest of them in the century to come was so great a man as he. Had he lived to encounter them, he would not have changed either his faith or his words:

'Mais qu'ont-ils vu, ces rares génies? qu'ont-ils vu plus que les autres? Quelle ignorance est la leur! et qu'il serait aisé de les confondre, si, faibles et presomptueux, ils ne craignaient d'être instruits! Car pensent-ils avoir mieux vu les difficultés à cause qu'ils y succombent, et que les autres, qui les ont vues, les ont méprisées? Ils n'ont rien vu; ils n'entendent rien; ils n'ont pas même de quoi établir le néant, auquel ils espèrent après cette vie: et ce misérable partage ne leur est pas assuré. . . . Ils ne savent s'ils trouveront un Dieu propice ou un Dieu contraire. S'ils le font égal au vice et à la vertu, quelle idole! Que s'il ne dédaigne pas de juger ce qu'il a créé, et encore ce qu'il a créé capable d'un bon et d'un mauvais choix, qui leur dira ou ce qui lui plait, ou ce qui l'offense, ou ce qui l'apaise.'

The argument has its weakness. To the notion of an indifferent deity Bossuet can only say: 'Quelle idole!' But on his lips the phrase is eloquent; it is the exclamation of instinctive repulsion: the protest of reason against the menace of moral chaos. The moral chaos was to come, and not a council of Bossuets could have prevented it. That reasonable order of things spiritual and temporal of which he was the last great representative was doomed; the moment was at hand, had indeed already come, when no man of his mental power could make the fundamental act of faith on which the great order depended. Perhaps Bossuet himself, in spite of Sainte-Beuve's easy dictum, found it hard. We shall not look, in such a man, for any more personal confession of his difficulty than we may elicit from such a rebuke as we have quoted; and, assuredly, it was not hard for him as it was hard for Pascal. There is no sense of strain in Bossuet; his faith was not 'a continual suicide of the reason'. For him, one such suicide, perhaps, but no more; one single surrender of the personal will to the great impersonal order which he saw manifest in history, and which he laboured so nobly to maintain.

It calls for a delicate discrimination to indicate the precise quality of Bossuet's faith. But, since all he was depended on it, the attempt cannot be evaded. There is no real approach to the sanity of his great genius by the road of mere literary appreciation. To neglect the theology of a theologian and praise his style is a solecism; where such a separation is warrantable, it is unnecessary, for there the style and the theology alike will be trivial. Bossuet the theologian cannot be put aside; for that is Bossuet the man. All the roads lead thither; it is the centre of the circumference. But Bossuet's theology, it may be argued, was simply the theology of Catholic orthodoxy. It sounds plausible, but only to those who are ignorant of theology. Those who are not know well that no mind that was ever truly orthodox was simply orthodox. Simply orthodox are only those who are not theologians at all; those blessed souls who have neither doubt nor the capacity for doubt. The late Samuel Butler would have been surprised to learn that what he launched as a *bon mot*—'There lives more doubt in honest faith . . .' is an accepted psychological truth; and Stendhal, who, as Mérimée said, could never understand that any intelligent man could be genuinely devout, would also have been astonished ('s'il ne craignait d'être instruit') to find that noi ntelligent man is, or claims to be, devout, in the sense which he assumed. The position is simple; no man can be a great theologian without a great intelligence and a great faith. These two can co-exist, though never in complete harmony, but the tension between them can become as natural and as vital as the tension between self-awareness and the sense of objective reality: the latter is the dynamic of life, the former the dynamic of the spiritual life. And even when man has achieved the slow but inevitable progress toward the complete identification of the spiritual life with life, the polarity will still remain: self-awareness will still be faith, though reduced by intelligence to a biological ultimate, and objective knowledge will still be intelligence, though infused by intuition to become a riper reason. Orthodoxy keeps the poles of faith and intelligence as far asunder as may be: therefore doubt is as necessary to it as is the overcoming of doubt.

The nature of Bossuet's doubt, therefore, if we can isolate it, will give us the nature of Bossuet. That he should doubt was necessary, so necessary that it does not at all conflict with Sainte-Beuve's description, 'l'âme la moins combattue qui fût jamais au monde', provided we remember that Sainte-Beuve was speaking of the earth's great ones. 'Moins combattue', relatively, therefore; 'moins combattue', infinitely, than Pascal: but in the ordinary sense, as Sainte-Beuve might have recognized simply from Bossuet's rebuke to the *libertins*, a battling soul. Listen, also, to the sequel of the same rebuke:

> 'Les absurdités où ils tombent en niant la réligion deviennent plus insoutenables que les vérités dont la hauteur les étonne; et, pour ne vouloir pas croire des mystères incompréhensibles, ils suivent l'une après l'autre d'incomprehensibles erreurs.'

There speaks to the discriminating ear not 'the least battled soul', but rather one of the most completely victorious over himself. And over his opponents, let us say clearly, Bossuet was also victorious. System for system, comprehensiveness for comprehensiveness, his was the truer: what perhaps he did not see, what certainly his real opponents (whom he scarcely recognized) were not inclined, or even able, to point out to him, was that they had no system, but took an ultimate comprehensiveness on trust. But even if this had been pointed out to him, he would have rejected them. He required a system and an order now, not in the dim future. While nations waited for a new order, crowned kings lost their heads and crude fanatics inflamed the passions of animal man. Bossuet's mind abhorred an interregnum, as nature a vacuum. It was monstrous; an offence to reason.

And so it is. The question is: what price are you willing to pay for order? Bossuet would pay any price, so long as the price itself were paid in order. Probably no man of the many who with him urged the revocation of the Edict of Nantes felt the grievousness of the stroke more than he, or more inflexibly demanded it. 'The man was noble.' And those of his Protestant opponents who could respond to nobility respected and even loved him. No Catholic polemist was ever more courteous or understanding than he towards the Protestant religion, as a religion: as system and order he was contemptuous and hostile towards it. What submission was required of a schismatic that M. de Meaux had not made? If he could make it, why not they? And, on the premisses, no reply was possible. Any position but that of a complete Socinianism shows as mere confusion against the lucid order of the *Histoire des Variations de l'Église Réformée*. This book is Bossuet's masterpiece: like the *Oraisons Funèbres*, it contains all the splendid compass of the man; but whereas in the Orations it is implicit, and only to be deduced by careful contemplation, in the *Histoire des Variations* it is explicitly unrolled. It is a great European book, and the book of a great European; in it a superb historian, a consummate psychologist, a noble humanist, a deep theologian are harmoniously at work. The reserves of force apparent on every page are immense; Bossuet, we feel as we read, can do anything. He is fair, he is even generous, to all the great reformers —to Luther, Calvin, Zwingli, and Melanchthon—yet each one of them becomes small and crude and pitiful. Towards Melanchthon Bossuet is positively sympathetic: in him he discerned the sufferings of a delicate and lofty mind that had sought rest in vain. All the pathos of heresy is in Bossuet's portrait of Melanchthon, whom, as he knew, he loved; but not for one moment does sympathy deflect the inexorable sentence, hinted on the first page—'grand humaniste, mais seulement humaniste' —and lifted into a profound and universal moral judgement towards the end. 'Chacun est maître à certains moments parmi ceux qui se sont soustraits à l'autorité légitime, le plus modéré est toujours le plus captif.'

But, modern taste objects, there is much theology in the *Histoire des Variations*. There is, indeed. Bossuet must be taken whole or not at all. That is not to say he must be accepted: but whole, whether for acceptance or rejection, he must be. Those modern devotees of Bossuet in France, who consider him mistaken in his attitude to tragedy, and would like his politics without his faith, have no right to complain when the sentence of Rome falls on them, as it has lately fallen. They are dilettanti, self-deceived romantics, who have played with fire and burned their fingers. How strange it seems that a man of M. Maurras's capacity should have imagined that the positivism of Comte and the political philosophy of Bossuet might blend! How strange that he could not see that a complete sacrifice of the ego was required by Bossuet both of himself and of those who would embrace his system; and that his own attitude towards it, of taking what was easy and leaving what was hard, was precisely the attitude against which the whole strength of Bossuet was arrayed. If we will not forgo our aesthetic values and offer up tragedy on the altar; if we will not forgo the values of our science and offer up the evidence of our senses upon the altar—then Bossuet is not for us. But to have seen that we must do these things, if we would accept him, to have recognized the necessity and to refuse it, is a more worthy tribute to his greatness than a more external imitation. To maintain that the Catholic Church is an excellent system of moral policing—for other people than oneself—is a form of heresy which Bossuet would have lashed more terribly than he lashed Manichaeism.

The price for Bossuet's order has to be paid, by those intelligent enough to admire it, by the sacrifice of that intelligence in its most secret home. Where it is most precious to us, where it seems to be knit up with our very being, there it must be offered up. There is no escaping the effort of faith in the individual soul. That is the corner-stone of the great edifice of reason which Bossuet maintained in its majestic integrity. Mitigate that act, as the reformers would mitigate it, and the edifice crumbles; declare it wholly impossible, as M. Maurras does, and there is no edifice at all, but only a moral anarchy where might is right. Bossuet, the great architect, knew exactly the position and nature of the stone which maintained the reasonable order of the world; and in no other of his works is his essential quality so nakedly manifest as in his simple prayer of preparation for Communion:

'Il est ainsi, mon Dieu, je le crois; c'est la foi de votre Église; c'est ce qu'elle a toujours cru, appuyée sur votre parole. Car vous l'avez dit vous-même de votre bouche sacrée: "Prenez, c'est mon corps; buvez, c'est mon sang." Je le crois; votre autorité domine sur toute la nature. Sans me mettre donc en peine comment vous exécutez ce que vous dites, je m'attache avec votre Église précisément à vos paroles. Celui qui fait ce qu'il veut, opère ce qu'il dit en parlant: et il vous a été plus aisé, ô Sauveur, de forcer les lois de la nature pour vérifier votre parole, qu'il ne nous est aisé d'accommoder notre esprit à des interpretations violentes, qui renversent toutes les lois du discours. Cette parole toute-puissante a tiré toutes choses du néant: lui serait-il donc difficile de changer en d'autres substances ce qui étoit déjà? Je crois, Seigneur; mais augmentez ma foi: rendez-la victorieuse dans le combat que lui livrent les sens. Ce mystère est un mystère de foi: que je n'écoute donc que ce qu'elle m'en apprend; que je croie sans aucun doute que ce qui est sur cet autel est votre corps même, que ce qui est dans le calice est votre propre sang répandu pour la remission des péchés.'

We have called it a simple prayer; but that is not the proper epithet for it. What is chiefly remarkable about it is its extraordinary lucidity. It is the prayer of a man who insists on keeping before the full light of his consciousness the nature of the act of soul he desires to accomplish. To many the act is impossible; but they should at least admire the intellectual honesty of Bossuet. He suffers no dubious half-light to make things easy, indulges in no ecstasy of paradox like Tertullian; he spares himself nothing. Obviously we cannot presume to ask how he succeeded; but we may be certain that he was not content with the mere words: 'I believe.' 'Dire: *Je crois*', he writes in the *Histoire des Variations*, 'c'est plutôt en nous un effort pour produire un si grand acte qu'une certitude absolue de l'avoir produit.'

This was Bossuet's fundamental act. By maintaining it, so to speak, at the maximum of lucidity and of difficulty, he was able to achieve the maximum of lucidity and ease in all that flowed from it. Granted that miracle, then the power to produce it lay in the visible Church alone; and in the foundation, the vicissitudes, the triumph of the Church, lay the meaning of history, and in its defence the political duty of man. The postulate admitted, the system inevitably followed. But we are not to imagine that Bossuet admitted the postulate because he so highly prized the system. The system was truth itself to him; it revealed a reasonable order in the world beneath an apparent chaos. There was no other system; therefore its postulate must be true. What was true, he must believe. Nor, again, are we to suppose that by a reasonable order Bossuet understood simply a political order; he meant no less a moral order in the individual man. They were interdependent: the one without the other an abomination. Knowledge of oneself, knowledge of the world, led alike to the same conclusion. The high mysteries of theology were ratified in the inward man. As for the Trinity, 'notre âme, si nous l'écoutons, nous en dira quelque chose':

'Elle est; et quand elle sait parfaitement ce qu'elle est, son intelligence répond à la vérité de son être; et quand elle aime son être avec son intelligence autant qu'ils meritent d'être aimés, son amour égale la perfection de l'un et de l'autre. Ces trois choses ne se séparent jamais, et s'enferment l'une l'autre: nous entendons que nous sommes, et que nous aimons; et nous aimons à être et à entendre. Qui le peut nier, s'il s'entend lui-même? Et non seulement une de ces choses n'est pas meilleure que l'autre, mais les trois ensemble ne sont pas meilleures qu'une d'elles en particulier puisque chacune enferme le tout, et que dans les trois consiste la félicité et la dignité de la nature raisonnable.'

The germ of the thought comes from Augustine, but how subtle and splendid the development!

'Il est donc maintenant aisé de concilier toutes choses.' We shall not blame Bossuet for his hardness towards Molière, or his tenderness towards Louis XIV. There is no reason to suppose that he *felt* hard towards the one or tender towards the other; no one can read Bossuet for long without being impressed by his essential humanity. But the order which he served was far above persons: it called for sacrifices at every turn. In that order Molière was not a great artist but the buffoon of an anointed king; Fénelon not a gentle genius but a bishop renegade to his high calling. The judgement which condemned them, though Bossuet spoke it, was not his own. We may not like the judgement, but it behoves us to understand that it was just. It was delivered not because Bossuet was harsher than other men but because he saw farther. If such a justice is intolerable to us, we can at least be grateful that a system which still fascinates many should have had a great man to make manifest the ruthlessness of its majesty:

> 'Cessez, princes et potentats, de troubler par vos prétentions le projet de ce mariage. Que l'amour, qui semble aussi le vouloir troubler, cède lui-même. . . . Il y a des âmes d'un ordre supérieur à ces lois, à qui il ne peut inspirer des sentiments indignes de leur rang; il y a des mesures prises dans le ciel, qu'il ne peut rompre.'

Order at such a price makes small appeal to a modern mind; for better or worse, we are become individualists. Nevertheless, the passion, or the preference, for a reasonable order in human affairs will not be denied; and, if ever it becomes predominant once more among men and is obeyed, there will be the same tale to tell. To make order we must make sacrifices. They will not be the same sacrifices, indeed, but they will be just as intimate and precious: the pound of flesh will be taken from just as near the heart.

Bossuet the artist—how horrified he would have been at the phrase!—is Bossuet the Churchman. Art there is, of course, and that consummate; but it cannot be held apart from the moral order which it was employed to manifest and magnify. Of art for art's sake, in either the trivial or the deeper meaning of the phrase, there is none in him.

> 'Je ne suis pas ici un historien qui doive vous développer le secret des cabinets, ni l'ordre des batailles, ni l'intérêt des partis: il faut que je m'élève au-dessus de l'homme, pour faire trembler toute créature sous les jugements de Dieu.'

He would have said the same of all his writings. To do that was for him precisely to be an historian; it followed also that history was for him the supreme art. It made manifest the actual workings of God. What could the art which we call creative be for him except the figment of an undisciplined brain? To allow it more significance than a vain amusement would have been to deny his own philosophy and make chaos of his order. A whole century and a half were to elapse before Goethe, Coleridge, Keats, Flaubert, and Baudelaire were to hint that art might be autonomous and supreme. What these 'romantics' did was to make of art the great sacrament. Once men of deep thought and deep experience had discarded the order of Bossuet, no other ultimate home was possible for them save the sacramental concept of art and the religion of immanence on which it rests. Probably Bossuet was incapable of imagining that such a fate might be in store for men; certainly it would have been for him a devilish abomination. But what he did see, with the utmost clarity, was that once the doctrine of the Real Presence had been surrendered then, ultimately, men must come to what seemed to him the abyss. That is the lesson, plain to read, of the *Histoire des Variations*. We do not take the lesson to heart, partly because we are a people of compromise, and partly because the abyss does not seem to us an abyss. We see no harm in being vague about God. We find nothing shocking in the dignitaries of the Church expounding a doctrine of immanence, because most people who are at once religious-minded and capable of thought are more or less immanentists at heart; and we forget that a Church is involved. Bossuet was incapable of forgetting that.

The abyss is of course not an abyss, provided that those who are in it know where they are and why they are there. No European writer is so capable of making it plain to them as Bossuet. In him they will find no vagueness and no compromise; rather, a lucidity and comprehensiveness which they can but envy and admire. But more than this; it is not too much to say that a study of Bossuet is a discipline most necessary to the modern mind if it is to make that self-consciousness on which it prematurely plumes itself real and complete

X

GOTTHOLD EPHRAIM LESSING
(1729–81)

GOTTHOLD EPHRAIM LESSING made one serious attempt to advance his worldly fortunes. In 1760, during the Seven Years War, he became Secretary to General Tauentzien, the military governor of Breslau, one of whose duties was to restore his master Frederick's finances in the good old way by calling in the sound Saxon money and issuing a debased coinage in its stead. Such profitable operations being full of pickings, Lessing had his chance, and took it, though not so well as the morality of the day demanded. But having money and being unused to it, he felt that it burned his pockets. Part he spent in collecting a magnificent library (which was sensible), part in playing faro for high stakes (which he said was hygienic). The hours he kept were in themselves deplorable; and they were vexatious to the good baker with whom he lodged. The baker took an odd revenge. He made a new mould for his gingerbread cakes, and had it carved with a caricature of Lessing dressed as a night-watchman, and his name in full—Gotthold Ephraim Lessing—below the effigy. Long after his death the gingerbread Lessing was still being eaten by the small boys of Breslau.

So runs the story: and it is symbolic. Not many men of letters have lent themselves to a gingerbread revenge, or achieved so queer an immortality. But in Lessing there was something of which gingerbread pictures, clay-pipe figureheads, or Toby-jugs could, not inappropriately, be made. He was solid. Between him and common reality there was a force of mutual attraction like gravity. He reminds one, in some essentials of Dr. Johnson. He might have refuted Berkeley by kicking a stone; and the sweat that ran down his face while he sat at the faro table has a sort of kinship with the knotted veins of Johnson's forehead when he sat down to one of his voracious meals. They had their feet not of clay, but on it; they were great men of letters, but we remember them as great men.

That is, if we remember Lessing at all. Even the *Laokoon* seems to be out of fashion nowadays, and to have become demoded like the piece of statuary from which it arose. We suspect that Mr. Irving Babbitt's *New Laokoon* is more familiar to the present generation than Lessing's old one. His discoveries have become commonplaces, his boundaries are landmarks. So also have Aristotle's; to whom, nevertheless, we pay lip-homage. But not to Lessing. Yet he was, of all the critics since Aristotle, the most truly Aristotelian; if Aristotle deserves our homage, as he surely does, so does Lessing—and in one sense even more than Aristotle himself, for he first showed the world how to see Aristotle as a master of method, not a mine of maxims. Since it is not an easy lesson to learn, we need not wonder that criticism has not greatly profited by his example. To use Aristotle's method one needs to be almost an Aristotle—and Lessing was.

He was, in short, a very great critic. Probably the greatest literary critic we have had in Europe—not in virtue of the *Laokoon*, though that is possibly his masterpiece, but in virtue of his qualities which are to be discovered everywhere in his work—in his *Dramaturgie*, and in those *Kleine Schriften* which Coleridge (to one's surprise) declared he read every year as a model of critical prose—and are so finely manifest in the *Laokoon*.

The chief of these qualities are two. One, which we expect naturally from so great a disciple of Aristotle, is a passion for clear distinction that never loses sight of the particulars to be distinguished. Drama and Art never become abstract for Lessing; they are always these dramas—and he seems to know all of them—and these works of art—and he seems to know a prodigious number even of them. He never talks by hearsay. The second quality is one which we do not naturally expect from a great disciple of Aristotle, not because it is not in Aristotle—it is in him abundantly—but because it is not obvious in the Aristotle expurgated by orthodoxy who is usually put forward for admiration to-day. It is a sense of the genetic and organic in things, and in the mind which strives to master them—of a creative *φύσις*; an attitude not at all to be confused with what is vaguely called the evolutionary outlook, or at least not to be equated with any facile version of Darwinism, but an instinctive or intuitive aversion from absolutes—a feeling that truth is as much a quality of the minds that seek it as of the things wherein they find it. The search is as important as the discovery, the method as the matter. 'The manner in which one has come to a matter is as valuable', Lessing wrote in the *Kleine Schriften*, 'and even as instructive as the matter itself.' And it was this sense of a dynamic governing the motions of the mind which made him so masterly an interpreter of Aristotle. He had, what Aristotle had, a mind so naturally comprehensive that it could, so to speak, begin anywhere; he was aware that approaches to the truth are many, and that all statements of it have an element of approximation. He held that it is by our power to hold various approximations together in a single act of apprehension that we show our capacity for truth. In this spirit he interpreted Aristotle, not in accordance with the demands of an impossible and unnatural clarity, but by himself; he did not regard the Poetics as an inviolable Scripture, but sought to learn how to understand them by studying the Rhetoric and the Ethics. It was the mind not the maxims of the master that fascinated him. He might have said of him what he said of Shakespeare, that he 'demands to be studied, not be plundered'. But the mind and the maxims of Aristotle were not to be separated; they were interdependent.

'I would seem to set aside Aristotle's authority (he wrote in the *Dramaturgie*) if only I could set aside his reasons. I have my own ideas about the origin and basis of this philosopher's Poetics, which I have not space to give here, yet I do not hesitate to declare (even at the cost of being laughed at in these enlightened times) that I consider them infallible as Euclid's Elements. Their fundamental principles are just as true and certain, only not so definite, and therefore were exposed to misconstruction. I trust to prove incontrovertibly, of tragedy in particular, that it cannot depart a step from the rules of Aristotle without departing just so far from perfection.'

There speaks not so much of the opposite as the superior of the dogmatic mind. The dogmatic mind reveres principles without understanding them; its opposite rejects principles without understanding them. Lessing was never, like the mere anarchist, afraid of dogma; he only insisted on understanding it, so that it was for him no longer dogma. This quality of mind is strikingly displayed in the *Laokoon*. To the casual glance, which is all he gets to-day, he appears to be reverential to classical authority. The matter in which his argument moves is wholly classical. It is only when we have begun to wrestle with the substance of his book that we discern that he is moving amongst the writers of antiquity as a man amongst men, discriminating, deciding values, accepting this as true, rejecting that as false, allowing nothing that he does not understand. 'We read fine things,' said Keats, 'but we do not understand them till we have gone the same steps as the author.' Lessing's ratification of classical values by his own experience is of this kind. He reanimates, and is reanimated by, the mind of antiquity.

That is why the *Laokoon* is a living book. The breath of life is in its style—swift, clear, colloquial, pungent—the style of a real experience, cutting easily and with a laugh through the tangled confusions of pedantic criticism. Virgil's Laocoon wears his priestly robe; the figure in the statue is naked. Why, asked the critics, this offence against the decorum? Because, they said, statuary cannot imitate drapery. 'The old artists might have laughed at the objection, but I know not what they would have said to this manner of answering it.' Then from his silver bow, Lessing lets fly his real shaft:

> 'In poetry a robe is no robe. It conceals nothing. Our imagination sees through it in every part. Whether Virgil's Laocoon be clothed or not, the agony in every fibre of his body is equally visible.'

How obvious! Yet no one had thought of it before. Nor even to-day is it by any means as obvious to criticism as it was to Lessing, that the application of the words 'imagery' and 'picture' to a work of literature is almost wholly a metaphor.

> 'A picture in poetry is not necessarily one that can be transferred to canvas. But every touch, or combination of touches, by means of which the poet brings his subject so vividly before us that we are more conscious of the subject

than of his words, is picturesque and makes what we call a picture; that is, it produces that degree of illusion which a painted picture is peculiarly qualified to excite, and which we in fact most frequently and naturally experience in the contemplation of the painted canvas.'

'Experience shows that the poet can produce this degree of illusion by the representation of other than visible objects. He therefore has at his command whole classes of subjects which elude the artist. Dryden's "Ode on St. Cecilia's Day" is full of musical pictures, but gives no employment to the brush. But I will not lose myself in examples of this kind; after all they teach us little more than that colours are not tones, and ears not eyes.'

That is, or it should be, one of the great commonplaces of literary criticism; even in translation it shows the easy vigour of Lessing's prose. Reading it, one can hardly believe that 'Ut pictura poesis' had reigned unchallenged for a century before it, or that it would have been possible after it for the confusion to lift its head again.

Lessing wrote plays. *Minna von Barnhelm* and *Nathan der Weise* have become classics of the German theatre. But he knew the real nature of his own eminence. He was, first and foremost and all his life long, a critic. Even *Minna von Barnhelm* was written rather to show the nugatory German drama how it might advance to some contact with reality than from autonomous impulse; and *Nathan der Weise* was deliberate propaganda for the cause which in his later life he had most deeply at heart. At the end of the *Dramaturgie* he explained himself and vindicated his own calling:

'I am neither actor nor poet. It is true I have sometimes had the honour of being regarded as a poet, but only because I have been misunderstood. It is wrong to draw such generous inferences from the few dramatic attempts

I have ventured. Not everyone who picks up a brush and lays on colours is a painter. My earliest attempts were made at that time of life when we are only too ready to regard inclination and facility as genius. What is tolerable in my later attempts is due, I know well, simply and solely to criticism. I have always felt ashamed and annoyed when I have read or heard anything in disparagement of criticism. It is said to suppress genius; but I flatter myself that I have gained from it something very nearly approaching genius. I am a lame man who cannot possibly be edified by abuse of his crutch.'

Criticism, as Lessing understood and practised it, was comprehensive and conscious of itself. It therefore passed continually into history, into philosophy and into religion. Yet he was, for most of his life, an ill-paid journeyman of letters; a journalist he would be called to-day, though it is difficult to conceive how a mind so universal would find expression under modern conditions of journalism. His fighting prose might be popular, but his seriousness and profundity would not. One can imagine well enough the general applause at some of his sallies. It had been written: Nobody will deny that the German theatre owes much of its improvement to Professor Gottsched. 'I am that Nobody,' says Lessing. 'I deny it entirely.' There seems nothing more to say.

But Lessing had another fling at Gottsched in the then new pages of the *Vossische Zeitung*, where he inserted this brief review of Gottsched's poems:

'The outside is so excellent that we hope it will do the bookseller's shop great credit, and we wish it will long do so. To give an adequate idea of the inside is beyond our powers. These poems cost 2 thalers, 4 groschen. Two thalers pay for the absurd, and four groschen about cover the useful.'

It would be cruel, had it not been so just and so necessary. The dilettante professors who composed cultivated Germany when Lessing entered the arena had to be smitten hip and thigh if a genuine German culture was to have room to grow. Lessing the journalist made fun of them, Lessing the scholar confuted them; and though a professorship was his only hope of security, he refused to join their ranks. The sheer strength of the man who thus, practically single-handed, cleared the path for German literature was prodigious. He created a public and imposed himself upon it; instead of the professor of a university, he made himself the teacher of Germany. 'What would you?' he replied to his friends who remonstrated with him for turning to hack translation, when the outbreak of the Seven Years War brought him once more to hardship. 'My writings are the productions of a man who is an author partly by inclination, partly by force. I cannot study at my own expense, so I try to do so at the expense of the public.' In this spirit, and by this method, Lessing pursued his task. He conducted his search for truth at the expense, and in the eyes, of the public.

But it was not until he was forty and had obtained the small security of a post as Librarian to the Duke of Brunswick at Wolfenbüttel that his dominant interest could fully reveal itself. This was religion. From early youth Lessing had been dissatisfied alike with orthodoxy, both Catholic and Lutheran, and with Voltairian rationalism. He had been educated to be, like his father, a Lutheran pastor, and he had very firmly refused. He had no patience with a nominal Christianity, and no intention of joining its *corps de garde*. 'So long as I do not see,' he wrote to his father at twenty, 'the foremost command of the Christian religion, to love our enemies, better observed, so long shall I doubt whether those are Christians who profess themselves such . . . .' From that bad beginning he never returned; but his interest in religion grew steadily deeper. He had only just begun to make his mark in Berlin when he went off to Wittenberg for two years, mainly to study the history of Christianity; and in his writings of that time the main lines of his future thinking already emerge. Heresies began to fascinate him, on the principle that, as he said later concerning Berengarius, 'the thing we call heretic has one very good side. It means a person who has at least wished to see with his own eyes.' And Lessing set about a series of rehabilitations (*Rettungen*). It was an unusual enterprise; but Lessing was an unusual man. He was himself rooted in and detached from Christianity. He could understand, experience, and sympathize with religious impulse and religious conviction: it never seemed to him, as it did to the fashionable scepticism of his age, an unintelligible aberration of the human mind. To such an attitude, a heresy was as interesting and as valuable as an orthodoxy, and from his study of the heresies Lessing gained, what subsequent students of Church history have sometimes gained, a passionate hatred of religious intolerance. But he was a wiser man than Voltaire; he never indulged the fancy that the way to extirpate religious intolerance was to extirpate religion. It was to purify religion—and this chiefly by two means; by insisting that the centre of gravity of religion lay not in theology, but in conduct, and by giving religion the courage to look fearlessly at its own history.

By these means he believed he was contributing to a development of Christianity that was inevitable. That the nominally Christian mind should be made to appreciate that an intolerant Christianity was no Christianity at all was an obvious moral preliminary to a religious or philosophical attitude perhaps not so obvious, but in Lessing's view no less necessary. This was to regard the history of Christianity genetically, and to be ever mindful of the fact that it had been manifested through fallible and imperfect human instruments. Already at Wittenberg, in a rehabilitation of Lemnius, he had applied this humanistic calculus to Luther. Lemnius had been, he discovered, the victim of Luther's violent temper, and historical truth had been distorted in order that Luther's glory might not be tarnished.

'I reverence Luther so highly that on consideration I am heartily glad to have discovered a few failings in him: otherwise I should have been in danger of deifying him. The traces of common humanity I find in him are as precious to me as his most dazzling perfections: they are even more instructive than all these taken together. God! What a fearful lesson for our pride! How anger and revenge may degrade the holiest! But would a less vehement spirit have been capable of Luther's achievements? Certainly not. Let us therefore admire the wise Providence that can use even imperfections for its instruments. . . . In fact, what does it matter what instruments God has employed? He does not always use the most blameless, but the most convenient. If envy was the source of the Reformation, would to God all envy might have such fortunate consequences.'

At the end of this essay was the sting. Since Luther was but a man, he concluded, there was no reason why Protestantism should remain for ever at the point of enlightenment where Luther had left it.

This early essay, with its dangerous or pregnant principle that all history is significant of the Divine purpose, provided it be read with eyes as free from bias as contemporary knowledge will allow, was itself a contribution to the further enlightenment of Protestantism. If that be granted of the past, Lessing was well aware, it must be granted also of the present which knows the past; and all that the human mind can do in the way of realizing the past is a necessary furtherance of the Divine economy. This effort to realize the past is the effort which gives unity to all Lessing's work. It is as manifest in his *Laokoon*, in the recurrent discussion of Aristotle in his *Dramaturgie*, in the archaeological studies of his *Contributions*, as it is in the religious and theological writing which wholly occupied the later years of his life. But to realize the past, for Lessing, was not to rationalize it; hence he was a baffling figure to contemporary rationalists. Reason and rationalism were for him two different things. Reason was nourished by the imaginative apprehension which elicited truth from facts; it was essentially a submission to facts: whereas rationalism was an attempt to tyrannize over them. Thus historical criticism, of which Lessing was virtually the discoverer, was the most appropriate field for the exercise of reason. Of true historical criticism rationalism was incapable, because it denied the validity, and even the existence, of many of the profoundest impulses at work in history. Reason was not afraid of mystery; nor did it demand absolute truth. Its delight was in the search for truth, and in the comprehensiveness with which it was pursued. Again it was at Wittenberg, that is when Lessing was only twenty-two, that he outlined his own ideal, in a criticism of the specialist mind:

'Everything outside his own specialism is small to him, not because it really looks small to him, but because he does not see it at all: it lies entirely outside his vision. His eyes may be as sharp as they please: one quality is wanting to make them really good eyes. They are as immovable on his head, as his head is immovable on his body. Therefore he can see only those objects before which his whole body is planted. He knows nothing of the rapid side-glances so necessary to the survey of a great whole.'

No single sentence better than the last could convey the distinctive quality of Lessing's mind, or his conception of the training and the use of reason.

The full employment of this reason he held, very definitely, to be a religious duty of man: *vitai lampada tradit*. In the religious discussion and polemic to which he devoted all the last years of his life, he came inevitably to hold a position unintelligible to nearly all his contemporaries. He had been, and he always remained, an admirer of Luther; but for Lutheran orthodoxy he felt a contempt which he was quite willing to express. On the other hand, with Catholic orthodoxy he felt the genuine sympathy that it could not fail to arouse in a man of his historical imagination. Such an attitude appeared merely capricious; and his bewildered Lutheran opponents ascribed it to a subtle diplomacy by which Lessing aimed at dividing Catholic against Protestant on the Aulic Council, and so avoiding suppression by the censorship. They could not see that an admiration of Lutheran orthodoxy was really incompatible with a genuine admiration of Luther. Lessing's perfectly reasonable claim that he himself was the genuine Lutheran infuriated them:

'The true Lutheran (he wrote in *Anti-Goeze*) does not wish to be defended by Luther's writings, but by Luther's spirit; and Luther's spirit absolutely demands that no man be hindered from advancing in his own manner towards the knowledge of truth. But *all* are hindered if one be forbidden to impart his progress to others. Reverend Sir, if you cause our Lutheran pastors to become our popes, to prescribe to us where we must stop in our investigation of Scriptures, to place limits to our investigation and to the publication of our results: then I am the first to exchange these little popes for the big one.'

That was written in reply to Goeze's appeal that the censor should forbid Lessing's publication of the famous Wolfenbüttel Fragments, the analysis of Christian origins which Reimarus, the Hamburg physician, had left behind in manuscript. With the publication of these fragments historical criticism of the New Testament began. Lessing did not identify himself with the theses of Reimarus, but he fought, in his most brilliant manner, for a hearing for them; and when he had reduced his adversary Goeze to silence, a great victory had been won for free inquiry, and a clear demonstration made that there can be no reasonable halting-place on the slippery slope of dogmatic Protestantism.

It was Lessing's clear perception of this which brought him into seeming alliance with Catholic orthodoxy, which has an equally clear perception of the ultimate destiny of dogmatic Protestantism, the difference being that Catholic orthodoxy regards as a danger what Lessing regarded as a destiny. The difference is great, but it is a difference of a kind that permits a clear understanding between the differing parties:

'I am more concerned [he wrote to his brother Karl] about sound reason than about theology, and I prefer the old orthodox theology, which is tolerant at bottom, because it is at open warfare with sound reason, whereas the new theology tries to bribe it. I make peace with my open enemies so that I may be better on my guard against my secret ones.'

Though in one sense Lessing was the father of the Modernists, it is easy to see from this statement of the situation that he would have disowned his children. On the other hand, he would never have admitted the cogency of the dilemma put forward by those who maintain that the only alternative to orthodoxy is atheism. He would never have admitted that he himself was an atheist, and no reasonable student of his life and work could imagine he was.

Nor was he a Deist. What he was cannot be easily defined. But the most memorable of his later works, *Nathan the Wise* and *The Education of the Human Race*, were devoted to making his position unmistakable. The main thesis of *The Education* was that revelation, in the history of the Christian religion, was an anticipation of reason —the means employed by the divine economy for inculcating truths too difficult for the unripe understanding of the race. The religious progress of the race therefore consisted in outgrowing the need of revelation. In more modern language, Lessing held that the great religious intuitions were prophetic of truths to be apprehended by reason. The final purpose of Christianity was to become unnecessary. With the greater freedom allowed him by the dramatic form, he drove home his point in *Nathan the Wise*. In the play the one genuine Christian is the lay-brother, noble-hearted and simple-minded. The Patriarch is a mere unscrupulous schemer, while the Templar passes beyond Christianity to an apprehension of universal truth, and touches the wisdom of Nathan. The bitter criticism of conventional Christianity comes from a Moslem, Saladin's sister, Sittah.

> Their pride is to be Christians, never men.
> Ay, even that which since their Founder's time
> Hath tinged their superstition with a touch
> Of pure humanity, is prized by them
> Never because 'tis human, but because

'Twas preached and practised by their Jesus Christ.
'Tis well for them he was so rare a man;
Well that they take his virtues upon trust;
But what to them the virtues of their Christ?
'Tis not his virtue, but his name alone
They seek to spread, that it may dominate
And cloud the names of other noble men.

'Never because 'tis human.' Lessing was, indeed, a humanist; and being a true humanist he was also perforce a naturalist. To the Christian piety of Daya, who must see a miracle in the rescue of Recha by the Templar, Nathan replies:

To me the greatest miracle is this,
That many a veritable miracle
By use and wont grows stale and commonplace.
But for this universal miracle
A thinking man had ne'er confined the name
To those reputed miracles alone
Which startle children, ay and older fools
Ever agape for what is strange and new
And out of Nature's course.

And when Daya demands to know what harm there is in their thinking that an angel rescued Recha, since with such a belief they feel themselves nearer to 'the great inscrutable first Cause of their deliverance', Nathan replies that it is

Pride, and only pride!
The iron pot longs to be lifted up
By tongs of silver from the kitchen fire
That it may think itself a silver urn.

A true humility was inseparable from Lessing's ideal of a religion from which all superstition had been eliminated. He detected—and his eyes were keen—a false humility in the apparent sacrifice of reason made by orthodoxy. True humility lay in the patient submission to Nature, of which man also was a part, and the illumination of reason which attended upon that submission. Religion, which cannot be reconciled with the intelligence, would have no difficulty in reconciliation with reason, for these were one. Lessing's life was a hard one, but it had the beauty which comes of deep inward coherence. He never took the easy way when one more difficult led straighter to the truth he sought. His work is a monument to the validity of his own unshakable conviction that not the possession of truth but the passion, the sincerity, and the tolerance with which it is sought, is the noblest achievement of humanity.

XI

THOMAS FLATMAN

IN late years two critics have done justice to the verses of Thomas Flatman, who was born in 1635: was barrister, miniature-painter, and poet: published a volume of verses which passed through four editions in the century: died in 1688, and was forgotten ever afterwards. The first of these critics was the late Mr. Bullen, who, when he said that Flatman was a serious poet in an age of frivolity, put his finger on the secret cause of Flatman's curious attractiveness; the second was Mr. Saintsbury, who, by including him in the third volume of his Caroline Poets and manfully proclaiming that 'he was a *poet*', has done as much as one man can do towards rescuing him finally from oblivion.

Now comes a university thesis from America on 'the life and uncollected poems' of Flatman which signally disappoints the appetite it awakens.[1] Apparently the reason for its existence is that the University of Pennsylvania possesses a Flatman manuscript containing about two dozen poems, of which most were published during the poet's lifetime; while an excellent transcript of the whole manuscript exists in England, and was properly used by Professor Saintsbury for his edition of Flatman. Mr. Child's only service to the poet is that he has published some three or four letters of Flatman to his kinsman, Archbishop Sancroft, which show that Flatman, quite naturally, had hopes of patronage from his highly-placed relative; and this small service is outweighed by the great disservice of attributing a mass of

[1] THE LIFE AND UNCOLLECTED POEMS OF THOMAS FLATMAN. By *Frederic Anthony Child.* (University of Pennsylvania Press.)

verses from the *Hercules Ridens* to the poet on no authority or evidence.

Flatman's name is unfortunate. Pope could not, in his most malicious mood, have named him better. At his worst, and his worst seems to have overtaken him more often as he grew older, he is just flat; absolutely, irredeemably flat; so obviously flat, indeed, that we cannot help thinking that the degree of his flatness was deliberate. When suddenly at the beginning of one of his later *Pindaricks*, on the death of the Duke of Ormond, he says:

> Fain would I pay my tribute ever due
> To his immortal memory:
> But what immortal methods to pursue
> Is understood by very few—

we feel that he is intentionally exhibiting his naked lack of inspiration; that he could perfectly well have disguised it, even though the disguise would have been thin to transparency. He definitely preferred, we feel, not to humbug himself.

Whether or not that clear impression of a sort of despairing honesty would be derived from those lines alone, it is certainly the interpretation we put on them after we have become acquainted with Flatman's work as a whole. It is a whole; and it is made a whole by the curious melancholy candour which pervades it. This appears, again directly, in the prefatory poem written in 1685 for his friend John Northleigh's book:

> Though I'm convinced of this, and right well know
> I can add nothing to your Book, or you:
> Yet I am forced th' old beaten road to go
> And tell my friend what wonders he has done . . .
> Farewell, dear friend! and for this once excuse
> The last efforts of an expiring Muse.

The thing is genuine; its disillusioned sincerity strikes us as real. We begin to touch hands with an interesting man, to respond to a temper which, in the crude but significant classification of the age, would be definitely explained as 'melancholy'. We begin to think of Burton; and we notice that Flatman too had great faith in astrology, and that a horoscope drawn for him, now in the Bodleian, is the source of our knowledge of the day and hour of his birth.

The melancholy man is there, lurking at every corner of Flatman's work. He is certain of the vanity of life, and he is not troubled by any illusions about himself or his verses. Sometimes he tries to be in the fashion and to sing songs which are light and gay. His hand is heavy, and he seems to know it. He is at home only with his own thoughts, and his thoughts themselves are at home only in the contemplation of death. Then his accent becomes grave, sonorous, and at moments trembles on the verge of re-echoing 'the large utterance of the early gods'. So, in his paraphrase of the famous little poem on the shipwrecked body in Petronius, he finds this unexpected stanza in himself:

> Consider well, and every place
> Offers a ready road to thy long home,
> Sometimes with frowns, sometimes with smiling face,
> Th' embassadors of Death do come,
> By open force or secret ambuscade,
> By unintelligible ways,
> We end our anxious days,
> And stock the large plantations of the Dead.

That is the very brink of the simple grandeur of great poetry. Something is lacking, it is hard to say what; perhaps it is the middle term of Milton's famous trinity —simple, sensuous, passionate. A passionate simplicity is never far away from Flatman, but the overwhelming sensuous imagination remains aloof; it will not visit him. He is serious, but he cannot quite overpower our minds. Sometimes his lines are astonishing, but then they are isolated.

> Nature and all her faculties retir'd:
> Amaz'd she started when amaz'd she saw
> The breaches of her ancient fundamental law
> Which kept the world in awe.

The organ-note is held only for a second, then is gone.

And again, in this also, we feel that Flatman was conscious of the heights he just could not reach; that he knew by instinct the tone of the utterance which must be his, or none at all. In *The Review*, a retrospect of his own life with a few queer anticipations of Wordsworth, he half-whimsically considers his own poetical defeat. 'To Poetry I then inclin'd', he says:

> Ere I had long the trial made
> A serious thought made me afraid:
> For I had heard Parnassus' sacred hill
> Was so prodigiously high,
> Its barren top so near the sky;
> The ether there
> So very pure, so subtil, and so rare,
> 'Twould a chameleon kill,
> The beast that is all lungs and feeds on air:
> Poets the higher up that hill they go,
> Like pilgrims, share the less of what's below:
> Hence 'tis they ever go repining on,
> And murmur more than their own Helicon.

Once more it is the odd note of genuineness which impresses us. Even Flatman's joke has something wistful, pathetic even, about it. He was not the kind of man who could make a joke; jokes with him too evidently serve as a kind of smoke-screen to hide from us that he is making the best of a bad job. He has been exiled from his own country. The gift that should have been his, the courage of the brave translunary things, has been denied him.

Our sense of Flatman as a poet *manqué* is part of his real fascination; but the deeper secret of that fascination is our knowledge that he was acutely and perpetually conscious of it. He was, as Mr. Saintsbury so justly insists, a poet; a poet, that is, by nature, by mind and temperament, from whom the gift of complete expression was capriciously witheld. Dozens of minor poets of his period wrote more nearly perfect things than Flatman; hardly one of them convinces us in the way Flatman does that he had the poetic mind. He was serious in the Greek sense of the word, which Arnold revived for us; he was conscious of human destinies; and the grave universality of his concern is for ever lending to his half-utterance, to his very flatness even, a dignity which he cannot wholly realize. So we read on and on, again and again, attracted by his very imperfection which seems so human, never quite certain that we may not be lifted into the upper air by some movement of impassioned simplicity. And surely we are lifted half-way by such lines as these from his ode on the death of the the incomparable Orinda:

> Too happy mortals, if the Powers above
>   As merciful would be,
> And easy to preserve the thing we love
>   As in the giving they are free!
> But they too oft delude our wearied eyes,
> They fix a flaming sword 'twixt us and Paradise!
> A weeping evening blurs a smiling day.

Because his response to mortality was real, and not

merely a formal pretence, Flatman's *Pindaricks*, in spite of their frequent prosiness and less frequent exaggeration, are among the best of that rather dubious kind. Flatman's general reflections on death may be commonplaces, but they are commonplaces which he has felt for himself. Sometimes vehemence, sometimes pathos, always a real dignity, can be found in some portion of his funeral odes. Even in his songs, for which a light exactness of touch quite foreign to his nature was necessary, he can occasionally draw upon a vein of quiet emotional gravity, akin to the solemn seriousness which always lies close beneath the surface of his odes. It is true that the one piece of Flatman's which is to be found in the *Oxford Book of English Verse*, the only piece by which he is known to the general reader (if indeed he is known at all), is called a song, and inasmuch as it was set to music by a Captain Taylor it *is* a song—but a dirge would be a nearer name. It is quite unlike what we generally understand by a Caroline song:

> Oh the sad day!
> When friends shall shake their heads and say
> Of miserable me—
> 'Hark, how he groans!
> Look how he pants for breath!
> See how he struggles with the pangs of death!'

The quiet emotional gravity which sometimes appears in Flatman's songs is of another kind than these convincing agonies, and can perhaps hardly be distinguished from that simple certainty of 'attack' so frequent in the minor Elizabethans. Flatman can never maintain the note. But if the rest of *The Indifferent* had been on the level of its unadorned beginning—

> Prithee confess for my sake and your own,
> Am I the man or no?
> If I am he, thou canst not do 't too soon,
> If not, thou canst not be too slow—

it would have been, what none of his songs actually is, a little masterpiece. When he fails he fails, as it were, in the daylight. He does not try to cover his own discomfiture in the mist of an accommodating vagueness. Take, for instancc, these lines from his ode on the death of his brother:

> But when I call to mind how thy kind eyes
> Were passionately fixed on mine,
> How, when thy faltering tongue gave o'er
> And I could hear thy pleasing voice no more;
> How, when I laid my cheek to thine,
> Kiss'd thy pale lips, and press'd thy trembling hand,
> Thou, in return, smil'dst gently in my face,
> And hugg'dst me with a close embrace;
> I am amaz'd, I am unmann'd.
> Something extremely kind I fain would say,
> But through the tumult of my heart,
> With too officious love opprest,
> I find my feeble words can never force their way.

At the first reading, 'Something extremely kind' seems hopeless as poetry; yet afterwards we feel that there is some necessary relation between the failure of his verse and the dumbness of his affection. 'Extremely kind' and all, the thing sticks by the candour of its unstrained sincerity.

There perhaps we have hit upon one of the epithets for Flatman. He is unstrained. He does not make the high attempt of the metaphysical—for his powers the effort would have been insincere, and honesty forbade. He is definitely not a minor metaphysical. On the other hand, he does not affect the airs and graces of the true Caroline; he reminds us of Wycherley's Manly among the town gallants. He does not imitate them, half because he despises them, half because he knows he could not if he tried. So he elects, having deep feelings, to express them on the whole as nakedly as his age allowed. Seeing that melancholy had marked him for her own from the beginning, his temper was at odds with the temper of his time. The one or two occasions when he tries to tune his note to 'Carpe diem' he succeeds only in showing that his heart is not at all in the business. Though he tried to translate Horace, Job and Lucretius were his natural reading; and, wonder of wonders, his metrical paraphrase of some verses of Job is impressive. Nor is it surprising that his two best poems, *The Review* and *Oh the sad day*, contain unmistakable reminiscences of that paraphrase. In his quaint little expansion of Lucretius's three famous lines: 'Jam, jam non domus accipiet te laeta . . .'

> No more thy pretty darling babes shall greet thee
> By thy kind name, nor strive who first shall meet thee.
> Their kisses with a secret pleasure shall not move thee!
> For who shall say to thy dead clay, 'I love thee'?

the simple insistence is, in its kind, not altogether unworthy of its great original.

Over and above all this, Flatman has the attraction of the man who has no illusions about himself: he knows. Though he imitates Cowley, it is not of Cowley he thinks when he acknowledges his failure; it is of 'reverend Donne's and noble Herbert's flame'. That flame which he envied he could not kindle in himself. Imagination and faith alike failed him. As he grows towards middle age we can watch in his verses his loss of interest in an art in which he cared to excel, and might have excelled, only in one way. And in this, we think, lies the final and enduring interest of Flatman. He is not a successful minor poet, nor an unsuccessful one. He does not really belong to the race of minor poets at all. He is a failure in a higher kind; and he is able constantly to thrill us, even though we know we shall be disappointed, with the expectation of some singular success.

XII

THE COUNTESS OF WINCHILSEA

Anne Finch, Countess of Winchilsea, was born Anne Kingsmill in 1661. She belonged to the great Hampshire family of Kingsmill. Her father, Sir William Kingsmill, died in December, 1660, four months before she was born. She had a brother and sister. Her mother, a Hazlewood by birth and also an Anne, was married again in October, 1662, to Sir Thomas Ogle. Lady Kingsmill was then thirty, and her second husband twenty-four.

In 1664, when Anne Finch was three, her mother died; and seven years later her stepfather, Sir Thomas Ogle, died also. No doubt she lived with some of her many connexions, who naturally brought her up to be married, and little besides. There is a perceptible tinge of resentment against such an education in her poetry; and seeing that her dreamland was one

> Where no dowry e'er was paid,
> Where no jointure e'er was made . . .

and that none of her childhood connexions, save one, have any place in her poetry, we may imagine that she was none too happy as a girl. There seem to have been no childish recollections on which she loved to dwell, although she was precisely the kind of woman who might have been expected to do so: and the very fervour of her devotion to Mary of Modena, to whom she became a Maid of Honour in 1683, suggests that the fatherless and motherless girl found in her royal mistress an object of which her affection had previously been starved. And this perhaps will explain the persistence with which her loyal lover, Colonel Heneage Finch, Captain of

Halberdiers and Gentleman of the Bedchamber in the same Royal Household, had to woo her—in days when eligible suitors were not lightly put aside—before

> his constant passion found the art
> To win a stubborn and ungrateful heart.

I like to fancy—and fancy here may legitimately be indulged—that two at least of Mary of Modena's Maids of Honour, Anne Finch and that Mistress Anne Killigrew whom Dryden immortalized, formed with their royal mistress something of a feminine cabal. They were, I think, a little down on men, and perhaps the notorious liaison between the Duke of York and yet a third Maid of Honour, Catherine Sedley—what simple and lovely names!—made them adopt, as it were in defence of their mistress, a distinctly chilly attitude to wooers. Anyhow Anne Finch was no heiress; and we cannot suppose that she aimed higher than the son and uncle of an Earl. Besides which, it is clean contrary to what we know of her character to suppose that she put him off in hope of something better. And what we know of Colonel Heneage Finch makes it certain that she could not have hoped for a goodlier man or a more loving husband. The probabilities are that she was, though not quite 'stubborn and ungrateful', as she afterwards made out in the self-abasement of love, discouraging and superior towards his advances. Beautiful I am positive she was, but alas! a little of the blue-stocking and a little of the man-hater, and she did not believe in making herself too agreeable. However, the Colonel persisted, and she at last relented. The flag once lowered, came down with a run, for in the register of marriage dated May 14, 1684, in which the Colonel truthfully described himself as a 'bachelor aged about 27 years', Anne Kingsmill declared that she was a 'spinster aged about 18 years', which was five years too little. *Corruptio optimi pessima*, will say the feminists at this shocking defection: but I, like Richard Burton in like circumstances, declare roundly that I admire her for it. There should be no half-measures in love, and if Anne Kingsmill went to extremes at the moment she first indulged in feminine arts, it was due not to misplaced enthusiasm, but lack of practice.

There can have been, in the whole history of love, few happier marriages than this one, even though it was childless. Thirty-nine years later, when Anne Finch had been dead three years, the Earl of Winchilsea (as Colonel Finch unexpectedly became) wrote against the date of his marriage in a little private diary, meant for no eyes but his own and God's, 'Most blessed day'. There is no gainsaying such evidence, even by the professional cynic; but it really does no more than confirm the witness of the poems themselves. If it is not real happy married love that speaks in the most intimate of them then one man's ear for the voice of true emotion is hopelessly at fault. The situation was, of course, a little unusual for an aristocratic couple in those days; though probably the fashionable literature of the time leads us to think it rather more unusual than it actually was. Certainly, Ardelia (for that was her poetical name for herself, given with an obvious, and probably just, allusion to 'ardent') was whimsically aware of a certain abnormality about the whole proceeding—a husband who

> by tenderest proof discovers
> They err who say that husbands can't be lovers,

and a wife who positively shocks Parnassus by demanding inspiration for a love-poem to her legal lord and master. Indeed, it seems to be true that Colonel Finch found separation even harder to bear than she did. For when she was at Tunbridge Wells for the waters in the summer of 1685, in pursuit of assuagement for her melancholy or spleen, he felt so lonely that he urged her to return. It was she who had to be firm, as appears by the only decipherable stanza of her reply:

Daphnis, your wish no more repeat
For my return, nor mourn my stay,
Lest my wise purpose you defeat,
And urged by love I come away.
My own desires I can resist,
But blindly yield if you persist.

This was in 1685, the year after the marriage. Anne Finch had left the service of Mary of Modena; but the Colonel retained his posts in the Duke of York's Household. So they lived at Westminster, honourably situated, though not affluent, through the brief and troubled reign of their master. It was, we may guess, in Westminster, while James was still Duke of York, that she heard 'unpaid sailors, and hoarse pleaders brawl'. When James became King and in control of the Treasury, the sailors had no need to clamour for their pay. He was, she declares in her elegy on his death,

Open to all; but when the seaman came,
Known by his face and greeted by his name,
Peculiar smiles and praises did impart,
To all his prowess and desert:
All had his willing hand, the seaman had his heart.
He, born an Islander, by nature knew
Her wooden walls her strength, her guard the naval crew.

Yet another contrast she noted, as a member of a Royal Household well might do, between the reigns of the Merry Monarch and his more conscientious brother, and she gives us a glimpse of her own past anxieties, when she writes:

> Weep ye attendants who composed his train
> And no observance spent in vain
> Nor ever with uneasy fears
> Contracted needful debts and doubted your arrears.

But the halcyon days of paid sailors and paid salaries were soon over. Three brief years and all was lost. James and his queen went into exile, and the Finches, their faithful servants, into disgrace and poverty. They became 'gentlefolk in reduced circumstances'. In some verses commiserating with Colonel Finch upon his gout, Ardelia explains that he was

> Not rich enough to soothe the bad disease
> By large expenses to engage his stay,
> Nor yet so poor to fright the gout away.

For many years he refused to take the oath of allegiance to William of Orange, and thus debarred himself for his honour's sake from all places of profit and emolument under the Crown. Instead of a soldier he became perforce a student of warfare, and in *The Invitation to Daphnis* we are given a glimpse of him poring over the maps of Mons and Namur. Retirement was forced upon them, but they were fit for retirement. They were dependent upon the kindness of their family and friends; but their family and friends were kind. And though one may easily gather from Ardelia's poems that at first the position of poor relation was trying, one gathers with no less certainty that the young Earl of Winchilsea behaved towards them as a sympathetic kinsman should behave. At last the unexpected happened; the young Earl died leaving no direct heir, and Colonel Finch succeeded to the title. He put on flesh—the notebook records his being weighed at sixteen stone—became one of the studious antiquaries of the time, and in 1717 was elected President of their learned Society. Three years later, on August 5, 1720, the Countess of Winchilsea died. In her latter years she had published anonymously her *Miscellany Poems*, and consorted with the great wits of the age, Swift, Pope, Gay, and Arbuthnot. It was said that either Pope or Gay satirized her in *Three Hours after Marriage* as a blue-stocking with the itch for scribbling, and she was also said to have given offence to Gay in particular by saying that his *Trivia* showed that 'he was more proper to walk before a chair than to ride in one'. All this dubious gossip is uninteresting. What she was her poems sufficiently declare; and, if we set her poetical gift aside, we find in her and her husband a very perfect example of a type which, though it grows rarer, is assuredly not yet extinct in the English aristocracy: true ladies and true gentlemen who do not willingly provide paragraphs for the gossip-columns, nor take up postures innumerable in the illustrated weeklies: on their estates, in town, in the Royal Household itself, which they generally serve at some time in their lives, they live sequestered; secret charities, unpaid services, flow from them; and the love and honour of a countryside flows to them. Their felicity is enviable, but not envied, because they have deserved it: in word and deed, in courtesy and kindness, they remember that *noblesse oblige*.

Anne Finch was truly religious. She tasted early the mutability of human fortunes; and as Bossuet said of Queen Henrietta Maria, 'Elle-même a su profiter de ses malheurs et de ses disgrâces plus qu'elle n'avait fait de toute sa gloire.' The *Fragment* plainly records the process of her soul, and in many other of her poems are unmistakable traces of a genuine contemplative piety. The good Bishop Ken was her friend and spiritual guide. Thus, though in virtue of the nature-mysticism which utters itself in *A Nocturnal Reverie* she has intelligibly been called the precursor of the English Romantics, she is romantic with an essential difference. There is no trace of pantheism in her attitude. That had to wait for Rousseau before it declared itself. And that same *Nocturnal Reverie*, which by the depth and directness of its nature-emotion so clearly anticipates the Romantic revival, contains at the end a line which makes clear the distinction between the Countess of Winchilsea's creed and that of her more famous successors. In such a moment of rapture, she says, 'the free soul'

> Joys in the inferior world, and thinks it like her own.

Doubtless, the Countess wrote the line to guard herself against being misunderstood by other people and by herself. We have only to compare the thought of the concluding lines of the *Reverie* with that of Wordsworth's *Tintern Abbey* to understand the distinction between orthodoxy (which we may, if we know what we are about, call classicism) and romanticism in the matter of nature-poetry. The world of nature, though she loved deeply, was still the inferior world for the Countess; the soul did not inhabit there. Only there were moments when it could delude itself into believing that it did. In her 'recovered moments' she remembered that she must wait 'till heaven be known in heaven'. The 'ineffable recess' was not approached even in the most ecstatic of her earthly thoughts.

But she was in no real danger of sacrificing this life to the next. She was acute in her own self-knowledge, and was quite able to distinguish a mood of depression from a spiritual discontent. Her curious Pindaric poem *The Spleen*, which is said to have been judged the best account of that elusive infirmity by eighteenth-century doctors, shows that she had discovered for herself or inherited the sane psychology of the orthodox tradition. If Cowper or Smart had had her religious wisdom they would have been spared much suffering, and we might have gained much poetry. It is the spleen, she says, and not true religion which causes morbid religious fear.

> By thee Religion, all we know
> That should enlighten here below,
> Is veiled in darkness and perplexed,
> With anxious doubts and endless scruples vexed,
> And some restraint implied from each perverted text
> Is but thy niggard voice disgracing bounteous heaven.

That is religious sanity, condemning Puritanism; and the Countess's religion was so sweet and wholesome that she could on occasion, as in the last lines of *The Apology*, be whimsical about it.

The genuine love of nature and the genuine Christian piety which controlled it both distinguished the Countess of Winchilsea from contemporary poets. Though it is not true that religion and the love of nature are necessarily allied (for religion can become predominantly intellectual), it probably is true that a genuine nature-emotion is in some sort religious: so that we may say that if the Countess of Winchilsea had not been pious she would have been a pantheist. It was a very good thing that she was not: for pantheism requires a stronger nature than hers to bear it out to the end. Orthodoxy remained her support, and nature her solace. Thereby she found much happiness, nor was she often tempted to overtax her poetic strength.

That was not great, but it was real. At her best she has an exquisite sense of nuance, and a simple felicity in expressing it. Such phrases as

> Silent as a midnight thought . . .

or

> Softer than love, softer than light
> When just escaping from the night . . .

linger like fragrance in the memory. They are a woman's phrases; and they have a peculiar perfection of femininity. For a slightly different and perhaps even more characteristic nuance, of beauty tinged with malice, we may admire the two astonishing lines from *The Spleen*:

> Nor will in fading silks compose
> Faintly the inimitable rose.

That is the *ne plus ultra* of feminine poetry; a perfect example of the Countess of Winchilsea's lovely gift, quintessentially hers because it is shot with her own contempt for

> The dull manage of a servile house.

I may be wrong; but I am inclined to believe that those lovely lines had an interesting sequel. They are the jewel of *The Spleen*; but that poem contains another striking phrase:

> Now the Jonquille o'ercomes the feeble brain;
> We faint beneath the aromatic pain.

It has been already noticed, I think first by Sir Edmund Gosse, that Pope borrowed the phrase for his famous line:

> Die of a rose in aromatic pain.

But what I suspect is that Pope's line came wholly from *The Spleen*; and that he, with his notable flair for the excellent, combined in his memory the two memorable phrases—

> Faintly the inimitable rose . . .

and

> Faint beneath the aromatic pain

to make his more spectacular, but less lovely, line.

Exquisite is the word for Ardelia at her best. She had a genius for the intangible. Surely nothing, in its kind, was ever better than *A Sigh*:

> Gentlest air, thou breath of lovers,
> Vapour from a secret fire,
> Which by thee itself discovers,
> Ere yet daring to aspire.
>
> Softest note of whispered anguish,
> Harmony's refinedest part,
> Striking, whilst thou seemst to languish,
> Full upon the hearer's heart.
>
> Safest messenger of passion,
> Stealing through a crowd of spies,
> Which constrain the outward fashion,
> Close the lips and guard the eyes.
>
> Shapeless sigh! we ne'er can show thee,
> Formed but to assault the ear;
> Yet, ere to their cost they know thee,
> Every nymph may read thee here.

It *is* a sigh, drawn out to a lovely, silvery music, lingering on the air, gay and tender, a song, if ever one were, for a lover to listen to his mistress singing in a shadowy candle-lighted room to the sound of a harpsichord. And the same strange, simple, and impalpable gift of identifying her music with her theme shines out unmistakably in her little poem to the nightingale. I do not think there can be any doubt that she wrote it while actually listening to the nightingale's song, or that she was speaking the simple truth when she said:

> This moment is thy time to sing,
> This moment I attend to praise
> And set my numbers to thy lays.
> Free as thine shall be my song,
> As thy music short or long.

Enchanting is the simplicity with which she captures the veritable voice, the authentic thrill.

> She begins. Let all be still!
> Muse, thy promise now fulfil!
> Sweet, oh sweet, still sweeter yet!
> Can thy words such accents fit,
> Canst thou syllables refine,
> Melt a sense that shall retain
> Still some spirit of the brain?
> 'Twill not be! then change thy note;
> Let division shake thy throat . . .

There is nothing in it? I am not sure that there is not everything. I can but leave it to the delight of others whose ear for poetry is not wholly unattuned to mine. But that the Countess of Winchilsea had a subtle and instinctive understanding of some of the rarest effects of poetical 'music' seems to me indubitable: and for a sort of external corroboration of this opinion I would call in evidence the fact that for the 'musical' theme of her *Nocturnal Reverie* she went unerringly to the lovely antiphon of the final scene of *The Merchant of Venice*, 'On such a night . . .'

These are the pinnacles of the Countess of Winchilsea's poetic achievement. *The Sigh* and *The Nightingale* and *A Nocturnal Reverie* at least should be in every anthology. And, for yet another example of what I have called her sense of the nuance, and one that has the added interest of showing that her preoccupation with the elusive was conscious, there are the beautiful lines which Wordsworth admired and extracted from an unequal poem:

> Deep lines of honour all can hit,
> Or mark out a superior wit;
> Consummate goodness all can show
> And where such graces shine below:
> But the more tender strokes to trace,
> To express the promise of a face
> When but the dawnings of a mind
> We from an air unripened find,
> Which, altering as new moments rise,
> The pen or pencil's art defies;
> When flesh and blood in youth appears
> Polished like what our marble wears;
> Fresh as that shade of opening green
> Which first upon our groves is seen;
> Enlivened by a harmless fire
> And brightened by each gay desire;
> These nicer touches would demand
> A Cowley's or a Waller's hand . . .

But, beautiful as it is, it gives us a glimpse of the Countess of Winchilsea's weakness as a poet. She is inclined to be diffuse, to add touch after touch, forgetful of her main design. In this she reminds us of another exquisite minor poet, John Clare. That is only to say, what no one would have doubted, that the Countess of Winchilsea *is* a minor poet. But major poets are few, and minor poets of so delicate an individuality are not very numerous. We certainly cannot afford that a mind so gracious, and a talent so delightful, should any longer be a victim of the iniquity of oblivion.

The same self-knowledge that is apparent in the sanity of her religion is revealed also in her power of detachment from her own poetry. Sometimes, it is true, she carries self-depreciation too far, and she may be suspected rather of seeking to divert criticism than of speaking the truth from her heart when she declared of some estimable and forgotten contemporary authoress that she

> Of each sex the two best gifts employed
> The skill to write, the modesty to hide.

If anything is certain upon internal evidence it is that Ardelia did not believe that a woman ought to be ashamed of being a writer. Modesty was thrust upon her by a masculine convention. She accepted the convention, but she did not like it. And though she was glad of the fact that she had kept her poetry to herself and her intimates, she does not allow it to be thought that she was glad of the necessity.

'It is still a great satisfaction to me [she wrote in later years], that I was not so far abandoned by my prudence, as out of mistaken vanity, to let any attempts of mine in poetry show themselves while I lived in such a public place as the Court, where everyone would have made their remarks on a versifying Maid of Honour; and by far the greater number with prejudice if not contempt.'

Perhaps, if her verses had been more in accord with the fashion of the day, she would not have been so reticent. Although she was witty, and although she could be quite effectively satirical, she was not particularly interested in being either. The attitude must have made her quite formidable as a young lady in the society of her day. Wit in a woman could be accepted, and returned, if possible, in kind; but to know that a woman could be witty, and yet rather despised her wit, must have been alarming. It called for all Colonel Finch's good-humoured pertinacity to fight his way past the barrier which a kind heart and an original mind had set about themselves. And she for her part was quite acutely aware that her mode in poetry was not that of the moment. She imagines the fashionable critic objecting,

> Oh, stun me not with these insipid dreams,
> The eternal hush, the lullaby of streams;
> Which still (he cries) their even measures keep
> Till both the writers and the readers sleep . . .

'Insipid dreams' is, very precisely, what the wits of town would have called her best poetry. Its tenuous, intangible beauty would have escaped them. 'Insipid' probably would have been the name even for those lines which I prefer to Pope's 'improvement' of them. (It was the age of 'improvers'; and Ardelia occasionally made efforts to 'improve' herself.) 'Insipid', certainly, would have been the word for most of her loveliest lines: the pellucid couplet on first love—

> That oft I sighed, ere yet I knew the cause,
> And was a lover ere I dreamed I was . . .

or on a calm sea—

> For smooth it lay as if one single wave
> Made all the sea, nor winds that sea could heave.

'Insipid' above all the prayer, which she knew had been granted, of her *Petition for an Absolute Retreat*:

> Give me there (since Heaven has shown
> It was not good to be alone)
> A partner suited to my mind,
> Solitary, pleased, and kind;
> Who partially may something see
> Preferred to all the world in me.

But 'insipid' would have been their name for Wordsworth also, whose genius finally created the taste for the delicate emotional simplicity which he enjoyed in her work. This simplicity is the simplicity of distinctly felt emotion. The Countess of Winchilsea's contemporaries were less interested in distinct emotions than in distinct ideas. Neither alone is sufficient to make great poetry; but great poetry was not being written in the Countess of Winchilsea's day. Hers, at the best, was authentic poetry of distinct emotion; and that will keep it sweet for many years to come.

XIII

WILLIAM GODWIN

THERE are few harder fates for a man of some genius than to be intimately associated with a man of more. He is remembered, but in such a way that it seems better to be forgotten. He is generally used by enthusiastic biographers of the greater genius as a piece of stage-property, a specimen of muddled mediocrity (if not worse) to set off the transcendant qualities of the hero. Leigh Hunt becomes the appendage of Byron, and William Godwin the hanger-on of Shelley. Byron and Shelley are romantic enough to be fascinating to the common reader, and their unfortunate friends, whose destinies were too closely knit with their own to be ignored by the biographer, become fixed in the general mind as literary parasites. No one, least of all the biographer, troubles to ask why it was that the man of greater genius found the intimacy of the man of smaller genius indispensable to himself. The bare notion of a reciprocal relation is excluded by the assumptions of hero-worship.

The picture is too romantically gratifying, above all too easy, to be dislodged from the general imagination. Even to assess a man of a minor genius is no light labour; and it is probable that nine in ten of those who permit themselves to dismiss William Godwin with a cheap sneer have not read his writings. He sponged on Shelley; and there is an end of him. That Shelley sponged on him is not so much forgotten as not understood, for that would demand that Shelley's poetry should be read with application. At a modest estimate three-quarters of it is Godwin in poetry. He gave Shelley his ideas and expected Shelley to give him his money. Was it really so monstrous? Or does it seem monstrous mainly to those for whom money is real and ideas next door to nonentities? Perhaps after all Godwin's chief crime is that he actually believed he had given value for money.

And the memory of it is apparently ineradicable. For what little writing there has been about William Godwin has been admirable. Not unnaturally, for Godwin cannot be tackled on five minutes' acquaintance. Hazlitt knew his writings through and through before he wrote his masterly essay in *The Spirit of the Age*; and in these latter days Mr. Brailsford had grappled him thoroughly before setting his hand to his small masterpiece of exposition, *Shelley, Godwin, and their Circle*. But the picture of Godwin in the general mind remains unchanged; nor will it be altered by Mr. Brown's valuable biography.[1] The one hope of rehabilitation we see for him is in a growing awareness of the charm and genius of Mary Wollstonecraft. When the vogue of 'frail' eighteenth-century ladies has subsided, one of the loveliest and bravest of Englishwomen may come to her own; and then a little of her glory may be shed upon the man with whom she found her peace and rest.

Even now it is through Mary Wollstonecraft that we need to approach Godwin. To look at him directly is to be puzzled. To find a common author for *Political Justice* and *Caleb Williams* is not so easy for us as it was for Hazlitt, who knew him in his habit as he lived. And the fact that Charles Lamb admired and loved Godwin does no more than make us sensible of the existence of an unknown quality. Godwin's own method of expression is so rigidly intellectual that we search *Political Justice* for traces of his humanity; until it suddenly

[1] THE LIFE OF WILLIAM GODWIN. By *Ford K. Brown*. (Dent.)

occurs to us that Godwin's 'reason' is the concept of a recluse, which in reality contains under one convenient label a whole host of instincts and emotions. He has done what most men do who entertain a like purpose—namely, rationalized his own 'values'. Godwin's 'universal benevolence' is not a deduction, but an assumption; he was trying to find a reason for the emotion which he felt, and the ideal of which he dreamed.

This surmise becomes a certainty when we read Godwin's memoir of Mary Wollstonecraft. The formal language of the philosopher there becomes merely quaint and charming, as he tries to subdue it to the tenderness of his love. He is unused to the melting mood. Twenty-five years of hack-work and solitary speculation have stiffened his writing arm. But declare the exquisiteness of Mary Wollstonecraft to the world he must, and will. And the issue of his courage is beautiful:

'When we met again, we met with a new pleasure, and, I may add, with a more decisive preference for each other. It was, however, three weeks longer before the sentiment which trembled on the tongue burst from the lips of either. There was, I have already said, no period of throes and resolute explanation attendant on the tale. It was friendship melting into love. Previously to our mutual declaration, each felt half-assured, yet each felt a certain trembling anxiety to have assurance complete.

'Mary rested her head upon the shoulder of her lover, hoping to find a heart with which she might safely treasure her world of affection; fearing to commit a mistake, yet in spite of her melancholy experience, fraught with that generous confidence which in a great soul is never extinguished. I had never loved till now; or at least had never nourished a passion to the same growth, or met with an object so consummately worthy.'

That Godwin was capable of feeling and inspiring such love is of the utmost importance to an understanding of him. The rational romanticism of such a *philosophe* seems remote and arid to a modern sense; yet we have to account for the truly prodigious enthusiasm his writings inspired in the most generous spirits of the age. Coleridge and Wordsworth, Hazlitt and Shelley—to have kindled such men to fervour is not an accident; nor were the enthusiasts simply deluded youths. Hazlitt, the toughest-minded man among them all, was loyal to Godwin all his days. Hazlitt also was the one who retained his own powers. In Godwin's memoir of Mary Wollstonecraft we have more than a glimpse of the secret. Behind *Political Justice* is a fervid idealism. Its apparent aridity was its crowning perfection in the eyes of those who responded to it, for it appeared to them, as it did to Godwin himself, an irrefutable demonstration of the validity of their instinctive beliefs. The good and the beautiful were true. It was as though he had proved the necessity of the Kingdom of Heaven by Euclid.

The closer we look at Godwin the less we are inclined to smile at him. Probably it does not do to be an idealist; it is to be reckoned a dangerous trade. Godwin himself found it so. But it is also true that the idealists are the salt of the earth, as the greatest of them declared. And there are moments in our reading of the preposterous story of Godwin's financial entanglements, which Mr. Brown tells in detail, when it comes upon us with a sudden flash that Godwin was just as other-worldly as Shelley himself. He seems to be living in a region of thought where he has a perfect and obvious right to the money of his friends. He has striven his utmost for the ideal republic; he has codified its laws; and he has lived in obedience to them. He has practised universal benevolence—few men have been more generous than he—and he expects universal benevolence to be shown to him. Unfortunately, instead of its being given spontaneously, he is compelled to ask for it. Very good, he will ask. His correspondence with Francis Place, who had busied himself trying to put his affairs in order, is illuminating. The two men speak quite different languages. Godwin has 'promised' to pay £300 on such a day. The money is not paid. 'But you *promised*', says Place. 'Of course I promised—to pay the money *if I had it*.' Place is disgusted, and Godwin genuinely bewildered. Who is to judge between them? For, let it be remembered, Godwin's admirers, who helped him with loans, admired him because of *Political Justice*; they professed to believe in the book. Was it unnatural that, in his dealings with them, Godwin should expect to be treated in accordance with its principles? To one who carefully reads the correspondence with Place, as presented by Mr. Brown, and is puzzled, as he is bound to be, by the tone of gentle forbearance, of patient magnanimity, which Godwin adopts towards his indignant helper, inevitably comes the thought that Godwin did really regard him as one who, through some deficiency in natural light, could not grasp the fundamental principle of 'universal benevolence'.

With Shelley the case is different. Shelley's real grievance against Godwin was not financial: it was that Godwin refused to countenance his elopement with Mary. Shelley thought that refusal was a treachery to the principles of *Political Justice*. Perhaps it was; but Godwin thought not, and he claimed to be the authoritative expositor of his own ideas. Anyhow, Godwin had married Mary Wollstonecraft before Mary Shelley was born: both he and Mary Wollstonecraft had come to the wise conclusion that it is futile to challenge society over outward forms when you have secured the inward reality. As Godwin characteristically put it:

> 'After the experience of seven months of as intimate an intercourse as our respective modes of living would admit, there was certainly less hazard to either, in the subjecting ourselves to those consequences which the laws of England annex to the relations of husband and wife.'

Even had Shelley been unattached, Godwin might well have objected to his daughter's repeating his own experiment. But Shelley, only a few months before, had been living with Harriet for his devoted wife, in Godwin's house. Not only was he unable to marry Mary when he eloped with her, but he still regarded Harriet as his wife, and when she bore him a son bade Mary rejoice with him. Godwin regarded this as an illegitimate application of the principle of 'universal benevolence', and, what is more, one calculated to injure grievously the reputation of his daughter, whom he loved, and of Godwin himself, for whom he was not without affection. His view was certainly not unreasonable. To exonerate Godwin completely in his relations with Shelley would be foolish; but it is equally foolish to represent Shelley as the sinned against and Godwin as the sinner, to award Shelley the large licence of genius and to judge Godwin by the standards of a commercial morality. Shelley lived, more extravagantly than Godwin himself, by Godwin's ideas. Godwin was poor, Shelley was rich; that was the principal difference between them in the matter of conduct. When that is admitted, we can make our choice. Either wag our heads with Matthew Arnold and groan 'What a set!' or allow that each made a courageous effort to live up to difficult and exacting ideals.

The only fault we have to find with Mr. Brown's excellent Life is that his detached and subrisive manner tends to overcome, in the final impression, the sympathy he feels for his subject. Godwin still looms before us as something of a monster; the apparent inconsistencies of his behaviour are not mitigated by explanation. Even in his worst period there was something heroic in Godwin's unremitting struggles to present a bold front to a constantly hostile world. He had to bear more than a man's share of adversity. He had written the most famous book of social theory, the most famous novel of his age; by a masterly pamphlet he had saved the liberty of the subject at the trial of the members of the Corresponding Society before Chief Justice Eyre; yet at fifty years of age he was forced to write children's books for a living, and to write them anonymously because of the universal odium of his name. He had loved and he had been loved by a noble and beautiful woman; after a year of happiness she died, and his attempt to pay a just tribute to her memory was denounced as the very extravagance of immorality. Yet he seems never to have been embittered by his misfortunes, but to have worked stolidly on, 'in the serene twilight of a doubtful immortality', in the midst of hopeless embarrassments, till the end. The more we know of him, the less are we inclined to pass judgement upon him; he was too perilously near being a great man. But one little mystery remains. Godwin's method of living was austere almost to parsimony. At a modest estimate he must have had from Shelley and his other friends £10,000. Where did the money go?

XIV

CRABB ROBINSON AND THE WORDSWORTHS

PROBABLY the best thing yet written about Henry Crabb Robinson is Walter Bagehot's vivid essay. In it we see and hear the man, forgetting to make the tea at his breakfast-parties, keeping his unprepared guests ('the more astute used to breakfast before they came') hungry while he made them 'undergo the bust', pointing his familiar anecdotes with an out-thrust of his chin. 'Old Crabb' is there, with his 'slovenly' nose, his inability to remember names, which gave Bagehot the sly excuse to convey in a single remark—a triumph of narration—both 'old Crabb's' tone and young Matthew Arnold's manner:

> 'Probably the most able, and certainly the most consequential, of all the young persons I know. You know which it is. The one with whom I could never *presume* to be intimate. The one whose father I knew so many years.'

But Bagehot is a little cruel; he seemed to have forgotten that 'old Crabb' was once young, and that the garrulous last twenty of a life of ninety years might not reveal, even to a critic of genius, the whole secret of a personality which great men had loved and trusted. Besides being a little cruel, Bagehot is also a little unfair. We would not willingly forgo the picture of 'the wonderful and dreary faces' which Clough used to make while he listened perforce to Crabb Robinson's reading of Wordsworth's poems; but we cannot admit the implication that the old man did not truly appreciate the poet, while the young one did. Both of them revered Wordsworth, in different ways and perhaps for different qualities; but

Clough's reverence was barely this side idolatry, whereas old Crabb had known, and knew that he had known, a greater man—Goethe. In our slightly changed perspective, Crabb Robinson's appears the sounder judgement.

Professor Edith Morley's admirable edition [1] of all those of Crabb Robinson's papers which are concerned with the Wordsworth circle puts an end to all doubts of his critical understanding of Wordsworth's poetry. It contains two careful letters written by him to a young correspondent who found the approach to Wordsworth's poetry none too easy. They prove that, even if, as Bagehot says, the old man did not read the best of Wordsworth's poems at his breakfast-parties—and Bagehot does not tell us which he read—he knew perfectly well which were the best. Matthew Arnold himself could hardly have improved on his selection. And Bagehot's suggestion that he was impervious to mysticism is pointedly answered by his brief comment on the *Intimations* ode:

> 'This is the grandest of Wordsworth's smaller poems, as it is perhaps the grandest ode in the English language. But let it be passed over for the present. It is, as some say, mystical. It treats of a mystery, certainly.'

Evidently Crabb Robinson was, like many other good men, shy of the word 'mystical'; he was mistrustful of high-falutin; and very probably he was not, as Bagehot hints, the kind of man to draw out the philosophical implications of Wordsworth's poetry. But neither was Wordsworth himself. One of the most critically valuable letters in Professor Morley's collection is one of

[1] The Correspondence of Henry Crabb Robinson with the Wordsworth Circle (1808–66). Arranged and edited by *Edith J. Morley*. Two volumes. (Oxford: Clarendon Press. London: Milford.)

Wordsworth's, dated 1814, carefully copied by Crabb Robinson, with a due sense of its importance, in which the poet struggles, vehemently and awkwardly, with the charge that he did not distinguish 'between Nature as the work of God and God Himself'. It is a charge which a precise theologian must inevitably bring against Wordsworth's poetry; and later on we find Crabb Robinson reporting to the poet a very definite condemnation of his heresy by a Puseyite clergyman. Crabb found, we think, a certain satisfaction in communicating the charge, for he had no sympathy with Wordsworth's evolution towards orthodoxy. And Professor de Sélincourt's recent publication of the early version of *The Prelude* has clearly shown how uncomfortable Wordsworth was about his own youthful Pantheism, and how carefully he tried to cover up its traces. But the effort, in itself not very successful, compelled him to do violence to his former experiences; and to this troublesome theological preoccupation we should probably ascribe the curious acerbity of his reply, at a moment when he was worrying about the classification of his poems, to Charles Lamb's very sensible and characteristic suggestion—duly conveyed by Crabb—that there 'was only one good order—and that is the order in which they were written'. To Crabb came the tart reply: 'L.'s order of time is the very worst that could be followed.' Lamb was quite right, Wordsworth quite wrong: and we may guess his ill-temper was due to a consciousness that Lamb had not changed and he had. A chronological order would have made the change uncomfortably evident. The theological question vexed Wordsworth; and he was not fitted to be a theologian. He shows himself, in the letter of 1814, impatient with his difficulty and eager to be rid of it.

'Whence does she gather that the author of the Excursion looks upon Nature and God as the same? He does not indeed consider the Supreme Being as bearing the same relation to the Universe as a Watch maker bears to a watch —in fact there is nothing in the course of religious education adopted in this country and in the use made by us of the Holy Scriptures that appears to me so injurious as the perpetually talking about *making* by God. . . . For Heaven's sake in your religious talk with children say as little as possible about *making*. One of the main objects of the *Recluse* is to reduce the calculating understanding to its proper level among the human faculties—therefore my book must be disliked by the Unitarians as their religion rests entirely on that basis and therefore is in fact no religion at all;—but—I wont say what—.'

That brings us back to Crabb Robinson, for he—if he was anything—was a Unitarian, in much the same sense as Lamb. But, in truth, he was simply a Wordsworthian: the difficulty was that he wanted to believe that the early Wordsworth was the real Wordsworth, and Wordsworth did not. Common to them both was a disinclination and an inaptitude for thinking out the theological position; but Wordsworth was resolved on being orthodox, while Crabb Robinson—in this, perhaps, not unmindful of Goethe—was content to remain where he was. Like a good many others, he preferred Wordsworth as poet to Wordsworth as Tory and High Churchman.

The deeply interesting record of Crabb Robinson's relations with the Wordsworth circle which Professor Edith Morley's volumes supply must be read in the light of this discrimination. Crabb Robinson had been one of those to whom *Lyrical Ballads* came as a revelation. Wordsworth had done something for him, and he never forgot it. Looking back, at the end of his life, when he had outlived all his friends, he wrote:

'A poem is worth nothing that is not a companion for years, and this is what distinguishes Wordsworth from the herd of poets. He *lasts*. I love him more than I did fifty years ago. You will see few men advanced in life who will say the same of Lord Byron, even though they once loved him, that is, as I did Wordsworth, from the beginning. . . . In my youth I fell in with those of his works then just published, and became a passionate lover. I knew many by heart, and on my journeys was always repeating or reading them. I made many converts. Wordsworth had to create his public. He formed the taste of the age in great measure. . . . The cause of the opposition . . . lies in the *simple style*, on which every abuse was lavished. Wordsworth was of opinion that posterity will value most those lyrical ballads which were most laughed at. He may be partial in this opinion; certainly they are the most characteristic.'

But ten important years passed between this first passionate enthusiasm and his actual meeting with Wordsworth, through the kind offices of Charles Lamb, in 1808. The admiration was as sincere as ever, but it was somewhat tempered: he could see the object through its cloud of glory.

'Wordsworth [he wrote to his brother] is a sloven and his manners are not prepossessing; his features are large and coarse; his voice is not attractive; his manners tho' not arrogant yet indicate a sense of his own worth. He is not attentive to others and speaks with decision his own opinion. He does not spare those he opposes; he has no respect for great names, and avows his contempt for popular persons as well as favourite books, which must often give offence. Yet with all this I should have a bad opinion of that person's discernment who should be long in his company without contracting a high respect if not a love for him. Moral purity and dignity and elevation of sentiment are characteristics of his mind and muse.

'As we were *tête à tête* I was gratified at being able to turn the conversation to *his* poetry. He expatiated with warmth on them [*sic*]. And spoke of them with that unaffected zeal which pleased me, tho' the customs of life do not authorize it. . . . Wordsworth quotes his own verses with pleasure and seems to attach to the approbation of them a greater connexion with moral worth, which others may deem the effect of vanity—I think myself there is a danger of his not allowing enough for the influence of conventional and habitual taste in making those dislike his poems as poems whose sensibility is yet awake to the moral truths and sentiments they teach and exhibit. He also speaks with a contempt of others which I think very censurable.'

Professor Edith Morley, in her preface, will not admit that Wordsworth was quick to condemn and slow to admire his contemporaries. She will have no spots on the sun. But no idiosyncrasy of Wordsworth's is better authenticated than this; and none is more frequently alluded to in the letters of his intimates and admirers, of which, together with his own, her volumes are composed. Edward Quillinan was emphatic about it. 'It was too much W.'s habit to be censorious of rival celebrities of his own day and too little his practice to give cordial praise to any of his literary contemporaries, even to those of earlier date. This is a great defect in him and abates his greatness.' But Crabb Robinson saw the defect in proportion. In his admirable letters to Landor, to dissuade him from publishing his satire against Wordsworth—letters in which his discernment is as apparent as his loyalty—he wrote:

'What matters it that he is insensible to the astonishing powers of Voltaire or Gothe—He is after all W.: In all cases I care little what a man is not—I look to what he is.—And W. has written a hundred poems, the least excellent of which I would not sacrifice to give him that openness of heart you require—Productive power acts by means of concentration—With few exceptions those only love everything who like me can do nothing.'

That may be Crabb Robinson at his best; but not a sentence in any letter in these volumes is inconsistent with that rare combination of devotion and detachment. As Tchehov put it many years later, he was one of those 'who are concerned with plus values only'. And nothing less than an unusual capacity for not losing the wood in the trees would have enabled him to maintain his intimacy with Wordsworth without sacrificing principles which he held as toughly as, though less stubbornly than, Wordsworth held his own. 'W. and I [he wrote in 1836] manage to differ without any acrimony—Were I not so good-natured a man as I am I could not quarrel with an adversary who seems to be made absolutely unhappy by the apprehension of a victory from my own party.'

But sometimes during his annual Christmas visit to Rydal Mount—'No Crabb, no Christmas' was the sentiment of the household—he found it hard work to control himself in discussion; and he would have to creep off to Miss Martineau or the Arnolds and let himself go on the forbidden subjects of political or Church reform. And occasionally in a letter, as doubtless also in conversation, he would permit himself the pleasure of pulling the poet's leg. 'I have gone so far as to say,' he wrote to Wordsworth in 1833, concerning his eye trouble, 'that I thought the Tories coming into office might do as much and more for you than any oculist.' Wordsworth instantly was drawn; the reply is magnificent.

'Now let me take you to task about a small matter. How came you to say, as you tell me you did, that the return of the Tories to place would be the best thing that could happen for my eyes? I not only have never uttered a wish to that effect, but have over and over again spoken to the contrary—my opinion is that the People are bent upon the destruction of their ancient Institutions, and that nothing since—I will not say the passing, but since—the broaching of the Reform Bill could, or can, prevent it. I would bend my endeavours to strengthen to the utmost the rational portion of the Tory party, but from no other hope than this, that the march toward destruction may be less rapid by their interposing something of a check—and the destruction of the Monarchy thereby attended with less injury to the social order. They are more blind than bats or moles who cannot see that it is a change, or rather an overthrow, of social order, as dependent upon the present distribution of property, which is the object of the Radicals—they care nothing what may be the form of Govt. but as the changes may lead to that. As to France and your juste milieu, it is not worth talking about . . . (and *I*, M. W., *will not* write another word on this subject).'

Mrs. Wordsworth's parenthetical ultimatum is delightful. It was also efficacious. Her letters to Crabb Robinson form the most charming portion of the book. Against her instinctive feminine sense of reality, her evident preoccupation with keeping a by no means easy house in perfect order and, above all, her feminine faculty for expressing personality as distinct from ideas in her letters, Wordsworth frequently appears like an amiable, shaggy, comical, stupid dog. That is, of course, merely the generic misfortune of being a man. It is not enough to be great to be proof against this wholly unconscious feminine criticism; one needs to be very great to have conquered, or never to have lost, that immediate contact with the actual world which women seem by nature to possess. We doubt whether Wordsworth, if he had been able to look down upon the scene, could ever have understood the true wisdom of his wife's action when she returned from his funeral to pour out tea as though nothing had happened. To him, who spent so many months grieving over his daughter, such acceptance would have seemed callous and inexplicable. Nor would he have understood, and probably he did not notice, as others did, that Mrs. Wordsworth's grief for Dora ceased with his own: she was concerned for the living, not for the dead. And perhaps one of the reasons for the affectionate vivacity of her correspondence with Crabb Robinson was that he too was something of a realist over ultimate things. When he hears that Dorothy Wordsworth has survived the crisis of her illness and may live on for years, he 'doubts whether this will be a good thing'; and, again, he writes to Miss Fenwick, at the time of Wordsworth's grief for Dora:

> Dear Mrs. Wordsworth is what she always was—I see no change in her, but that the wrinkles of her careworn countenance are somewhat deeper. . . . Poor Miss W. I thought sunk still deeper in insensibility. By the bye, Mrs. W. says that almost the only enjoyment Mr. W. seems to feel is in his attendance on her—and that her death would be to him a sad calamity! ! !
>
> 'I cannot help reproaching myself for my inability to conceive this state of mind distinctly.'

Keats once described Wordsworth as a master of 'the egotistical sublime'; and certainly there was in his composition a curious emotional egotism. The stern psychologist might say with some reason that he ruined the lives of his sister and his daughter by regarding them as appanages of his own sensibility. The more deeply we consider the exorbitance of his demands upon his womenfolk, the more we come to admire the flexible strength of his wife. We find one epithet recurring in the opinions of her intimates: she was 'wise'. Her wisdom pervades these volumes. It is elusive, difficult to capture in a quotation; but perhaps a paragraph from one of Quillinan's letters to Robinson will convey an idea of what it was. It is *à propos* of Harriet Martineau's anonymous volume *Life in a Sick Room.*

'They—all the Rydalites—Mr. Wordsworth, Mrs. Wordsworth, and Miss Fenwick, have been quite charmed, affected, and instructed by the Invalid's volume, sent down by Moxon, who kept his secret like a man: But a Woman found it out, for all *that*—found *you* out, Mr. Sly-boots! Mrs. Wordsworth, after a few pages were read, at once pronounced it to be Miss Martineau's production, and concluded that you knew all about it, and caused it to be sent hither. . . . Mr. Wordsworth praised it with more unreserve, I may say with more *earnestness*, than is usual with him; the serene and heavenly-minded Miss Fenwick was prodigal of her admiration; but Mrs. Wordsworth's was the crowning praise—she said, and you know how she would say it, "I wish I had read exactly such a book as that years ago".'

We can almost hear it ourselves. Crabb Robinson was the man to understand her; and she understood him. She gave him domestic commissions in London for soap and candles—these last very complicated—and we may be sure he executed them with precision. He took a world of pains in finding out, after each annual visit, precisely what present would be acceptable not to her, but to her house; and the house creeps charmingly in to her instruction:

'If it should fall in your way to pick up *for me*, *dog cheap*, the Quarto Ed. of the Lay of the Last Minstrel, and of Rokeby—I should be well pleased—as I do not think that these should *not* be found in a Poet's house.'

These were things Crabb Robinson understood but the poet did not; Mrs. Wordsworth could therefore write to him with a careless spontaneity that is altogether enchanting; and there is something characteristic of their relation in her sending him, at the end of her life, when all the Rydalites were dead, six pairs of socks, 'which she hopes you will value, not so much for any service you may have from them as that they are the knitting of your blind old friend'.

Crabb Robinson had many commissions from the poet, too: he was continually in request for advice concerning investments, and he was required to transact Wordsworth's business with his broker. These instructions he performed scrupulously, with a due sense of the honour conferred upon him. But Wordsworth seems scarcely to have regarded him as a person; probably it was not easy for him so to regard anybody. Crabb Robinson felt no resentment. His conception of himself as one 'who loved everything and therefore could do nothing' came usefully to his aid. But personal affection was what he felt and valued; betrayal of friendship was ever for him the worst of crimes. In the letter to Landor from which we have already quoted he became vehement.

'Since you use the word detest allow me to say that I detest nothing but malignity and wilful injustice stimulated by malignity—I detested Lord B: for his passions were all of an evil kind—vain, selfish, envious, and full of hate—he was in literature what Buon: was in politics—Both men of vast power—I hated Hazlitt and broke off acquaintance with him for his base and ungrateful conduct towards W. and S.'

He hated hatred with all his heart. Towards the end of his essay Bagehot describes how on two occasions 'old Crabb' nearly quarrelled with him—

'once for writing in favour of Louis Napoleon, which, as he had caught in Germany a thorough antipathy to the first

Napoleon, seemed to him quite wicked; and next for my urging that Hazlitt was a much greater writer than Charles Lamb—a harmless opinion which I still hold, but which Mr. Robinson met with this outburst, "You, sir, YOU prefer the works of that scoundrel, that odious, that malignant writer, to the exquisite essays of that angelic creature!" I protested that there was no evidence that angels could write particularly well; but it was in vain, and it was some time before he forgave me. Some persons who casually encountered peculiarities like these did not always understand them.'

Neither did Bagehot. He did not know of the letter to Landor. He could not have understood the cause of Crabb Robinson's enduring detestation of Buonaparte and Hazlitt. But the unconsciousness of his account of what seemed to him an old man's idiosyncrasy makes it a more striking testimony to Crabb Robinson's staunchness. The haters he once had hated he hated to the end. He cared for persons, not principles. He had the mind to recognize great men; but, more rare, the heart to love them. Like a true lover he could keep his eyes fixed not on what they were not, but on what they were. It was no wonder that great men were glad of him.

NOTES

Page 9. An essay on the sonnet *On First Looking into Chapman's Homer* (*Studies in Keats*) contains a detailed demonstration of the poetic process described here.

Page 22. I have since found that this suggestion is confirmed by Schiller's dictum, quoted with approval by Nietzsche, himself no mean poet, in *The Birth of Tragedy* (English translation, edited by Dr. Oscar Levy, p. 45):

'Schiller has enlightened us concerning his poetic procedure by a psychological observation, inexplicable to himself, yet not apparently open to any objection. He acknowledges that, in the state preparatory to the creation of poetry, he had not before him or within him a series of images with a corresponding causal sequence of thoughts, but rather "a musical mood". ("The perception with me is at first without a clear and definite object; this forms itself later. A certain musical mood of mind precedes, and only after this does the poetical idea follow with me.") '

Page 42. Those who have had the patience to make themselves familiar with Blake's symbols—a patience most richly rewarded, notwithstanding the contrary opinion of Mr. J. C. Squire—will know a more precise and more satisfying language than mine for expressing the distinctions and relations adumbrated in this essay. Reason, in the sense in which I use it in this essay, is the creative harmony of Blake's fourfold man. And the usurpation of control by the Intelligence is precisely that Tyranny of Urizen which is one of the main themes of his prophetic books. What I have tried to say in the concluding pages of this essay is said, more pregnantly, by Blake in seven lines of *Milton* (p. 46):

> All that can be annihilated must be annihilated
> That the Children of Jerusalem may be saved from slavery.
> There is a Negation, & there is a Contrary:
> The Negation must be destroy'd to redeem the Contraries.
> The Negation is the Spectre, the Reasoning Power in Man:
> This is a false Body, an Incrustation over my Immortal
> Spirit, a Selfhood which must be put off & annihilated alway.

This work of liberation is, for Blake, the work of the Poetic Genius. And it is a principle with Blake that 'the Poetic Genius is the true Man, and that the body or outward form of Man is derived from the Poetic Genius' (*All Religions are One*). This truth Blake afterwards expressed by saying 'The Imagination is not a State: it is the Human Existence itself' (*Milton*, p. 35).

Page 61. 'Eternity is in love with the productions of time', says Blake; and again more magnificently, with all 'the grandeur of Inspiration' when Los had entered his soul:

I in Six Thousand Years walk up & down; for not one Moment
Of Time is lost, nor one Event of Space unpermanent;
But all remain; every fabric of Six Thousand Years
Remains permanent: tho' on the Earth, where Satan
Fell and was cut off, all things vanish & are seen no more,
They vanish not from me & mine; we guard them first & last.
The generations of men run on in the tide of Time,
But leave their destin'd lineaments permanent for ever & ever.
(*Milton*, p. 20.)

Page 123. The famous Sonnet CVII runs thus:

Not mine owne feares, nor the prophetick soule
Of the wide world, dreaming on things to come,
Can yet the lease of my true love controule,
Supposed as forfeit to a confined doome.
The mortal Moone hath her eclipse indur'de,
And the sad Augurs mock their own presage,
Incertainties now crowne them-selves assur'de,
And peace proclaimes olives of endless age.
Now with the drops of this most balmie time
My love lookes fresh, and death to me subscribes,
Since spight of him I'll live in this poore rime,
While he insults ore dull and speachlesse tribes.
And thou in this shalt find thy monument
When tyrants' crests and tombs of brasse are spent.

This sonnet is generally supposed to contain a specific reference to the death of Elizabeth, and the liberation from prison of the Earl of Southampton, which occurred on James's accession.

The question is of importance, chiefly because Sonnet CVII is squarely and firmly set among a number of sonnets (100–12) which are obviously connected, so that if it must be dated as late as 1603 it is either necessary to date some of the adjoining sonnets equally late—which involves us in serious difficulties—or we must conclude, against the evidence of our senses, that this group of sonnets is a mere hotch-potch arranged in any order. It is worth while, therefore, to examine the sonnet carefully, and in its context.

Sonnets C–CIII all have a similar burden. The poet apologizes for his recent neglect to write in praise of his friend. His excuses are various and fanciful. In Sonnet CIV he tells how his love for his friends has lasted now three full years. In Sonnet CV he apologizes for always sticking to the one theme: the beauty, the kindness, and the loyalty of his friend. Which comes, very naturally, at a moment when he is trying to rouse his Muse again. In CVI he declares that all beauties sung by poets of the olden time prefigured the beauty of his friend; but he, who has the prophesied reality before him, lacks a tongue to praise it duly.

The order of these seven preceding sonnets is eminently natural, as will be evident to any one who reads them with care and responsiveness. We will omit the disputed Sonnet CVII for the moment and proceed.

Sonnet CVIII asks, 'Is there anything more he *can* write to express either his own love, or his friend's deserts?' Yet he must go on repeating his song like the Lord's Prayer. Their love, though old, is young. Where one would have expected it to die, it lives on undiminished.

Sonnet CIX opens a new theme. Shakespeare replies to definite reproaches of his friend for neglecting him—a neglect which naturally seems to be that for which Shaksepeare excused himself in Sonnets C–CIII. He now confesses that absence did 'seem to qualify his flame', but denies that he was disloyal at heart. CX–CXII, famous sonnets all of them, confess that he had, during this absence, 'made old offences of affections new', that 'public means' had bred in him 'public manners', and he sighs 'to be renewed'. But he cares not what men say, now that 'the love and pity' of his friend fill the impression

Which vulgar scandal stamped upon my brow.

At this point a well-defined and extremely important group of sonnets ends. This group of sonnets is quite coherent. The sequence is natural, the psychological process revealed convincing. First, an acknowledgement that his poetry in praise of his friend had dropped off; then a backward look over the three years of their friendship; then, a certain embarrassment at beginning his sonnets again; then, Sonnet CVII; then a delighted but slightly wondering recognition that their love had lasted, though length of time and appearances would point against it; then an embarrassed confession of disloyalty in absence, and of scandal which his friend's love has forgiven. The story is clear enough. An absence, a neglect to write poetry about his friend, a fear that his friend would not forgive, a meeting, a delighted discovery that his friend was still fond of him, and an awkward—but moving—defence of himself for his apparent defection. In this story Sonnet CVII appears at a crucial point. Does it belong to it, or not? It seems evident that it does.

But first let us observe a detail of vocabulary. The word 'confined' appears in three sonnets of this little group and nowhere else in the whole of the sonnets. The detail is of some importance. It not only points to the sonnets having been composed at the same time; but it gives a hint towards the interpretation of the word in Sonnet CVII, which is much disputed. "Confined" in Sonnet CV: 'my verse to constancy confined', and in Sonnet CX: 'A God in love, to whom I am confined'—clearly means 'limited'. There is no sense of irksomeness in the limitation, no hint of imprisonment.

With this preparation we may undertake the interpretation of the first four lines of Sonnet CVII:

> Not mine owne feares, nor the prophetick soule
> Of the wide world, dreaming on things to come,
> Can yet the lease of my true love controule,
> Supposed as forfeit to a confined doome.

Naturally, indeed obviously if we have regard to Shakespeare's fondness for legal phrases, it is 'the lease of my true love' and not 'my true love' which has been 'supposed as forfeit'. We may compare, among many other parallels, (1) 'This bond is forfeit'; (2) 'My bonds in thee are all determinate'; (3) 'So should that beauty which you hold in lease Find no determination'. A lease is not subject to imprisonment, but it is always subject to determination; and 'determination' is precisely the meaning here of 'a confined doom', i.e. a sentence of limitation. To imagine that ll. 3–4 mean that Shakespeare's friend has been supposed condemned to imprisonment for life is to show ignorance of the language of the sonnets and a complete neglect of the context of this one in particular. Shakespeare's fears have already been amply explained by the preceding sonnets: he feared, and had good reason for fearing, that the love between him and his friend was at an end. He had indeed supposed it as forfeit to a confined doom. The words are exactly paraphrased by the concluding couplet of the next Sonnet, CVIII.

> Finding the first conceit of love there bred
> *Where time and outward form would show it dead.*

Thus the meaning of the first four lines seems certain. 'Neither my own apprehensions of its decease, nor even the prophetic dreams of the world-soul itself, can yet set a term to the lease of my true love, which has been supposed to be at an end.'

The 'mortal Moone' of the next four lines has been generally supposed to be Queen Elizabeth. It needs to be emphasized that, if the 'mortal Moon' is the Queen, the natural meaning of

> The mortal Moone hath her eclipse indur'de

is not: 'The Queen is dead', but 'The Queen has recovered'. The normal meaning of 'endure' in Shakespeare is 'to suffer and survive'. You endure torments in Shakespeare's language; you do not endure death. The natural meaning of the line, leaving aside the probable reference to Elizabeth, is: 'The mortal Moon has been obscured and now shines as bright as ever', and that meaning is confirmed by the next line:

> And the sad Augurs mock their own presage.

Why, unless the moon had recovered from eclipse, should the augurs *mock* their own presage? Otherwise we must suppose they had prophesied prosperity, and were now despondently jeering at their own mistake. Such an interpretation hopelessly conflicts with the following two lines:

> Incertainties now crowne them-selves assur'de
> And peace proclaimes olives of endless age.

The conclusion is that if (as is probable) the reference is to the Queen, it is to her happy recovery, not her death.

The next lines:

> Now with the drops of this most balmie time
> My love lookes fresh,

mean, simply, 'this time of happiness is like the elixir of youth to my passion'.

> and death to me subscribes
> Since spight of him I'll live in this poore rime
> While he insults ore dull and speachlesse tribes.

As my love has triumphed over a threatened death, 'so I have also my own particular triumph over him, in the immortality of my poems'.

> And thou in this shalt find thy monument
> When tyrants' crests and tombs of brasse are spent.

'So, too, my friend triumphs over death in this verse of mine.'

The sonnet thus appears perfectly coherent in itself, and perfectly appropriate in its context. Indeed, the best commentary on it is contained in the surrounding sonnets. The substance of it can be reduced to 'Our love which threatened to die has survived, and no one dares to set a term to it. Just as the Queen herself has recovered from the death which was prophesied for her, and the uncertainties of the greater world are resolved in peace, so our love has recovered and has renewed its youth. Just as our love has survived the threat by death, so we, the two lovers, have each our separate victory over death, I as the writer, he as the hero, of these poems.'

If, thus interpreted, it is read in its place in the sequence of Sonnets C–CXII, it seems not difficult to read the story.

It is now three years since Shakespeare met his friend. Shakespeare has been absent a long while; in his absence he has made new friendships, encountered infatuations even, and his flow of sonnets in praise of his friend and their love has been slackened. The friend reminds him of this loss of ardour; and Shakespeare, with an embarrassed conscience, begins again. He feels at once guilty and grateful; guilty, that he has deserved the reminder, and grateful for the proof of his friend's constancy that it gives. They meet again, and to Shakespeare's surprise and joy all is as it was between them: the golden years return. But, when the first joy of meeting is over, Shakespeare has to submit to the just reproaches of his friend, for his behaviour during absence: he excuses himself by saying—with deadly seriousness—that his behaviour is due to his discredited and discreditable profession.

I have been concerned to establish a positive and a negative case. The positive case is that the sonnet fits with perfect appropriateness in its context. The negative case is twofold, namely, that it is unnatural, and does violence to Shakespeare's language to interpret (1) ll. 3–4 as meaning: 'it has been supposed that my friend would die in gaol' and (2) l. 5 as meaning 'Queen Elizabeth is dead'.

The positive and negative issues are interdependent: for if it could be established that l. 5 means 'The Queen is dead', it follows that the date of the sonnet is 1603 and the period of just over three years given to the friendship begins in 1599—to me a non-sensical date.

If we suppose that the friend is Southampton, as I do, the beginning of the friendship was probably in 1593—the year of the dedication of *Venus and Adonis*. That would give, if my interpretation of the sonnet is correct, about 1596 for the date of it. On grounds of style, that date is convincing to me.

Shortly after the foregoing note was written, Mr. G. B. Harrison, in a letter to *The Times Literary Supplement*, showed that in the year 1596 Queen Elizabeth was ill, and that her illness caused great alarm in England; further, that peace was established in France. The complete agreement of Mr. Harrison's purely historical argument, with the conclusions here independently drawn from the internal evidence of the sonnets, is striking.